Bluegrass Harmonica

By Mike Stevens

I would like to thank my wife Jane, my son Colin and Jim & Jesse for their help with this book.

This book is dedicated in memory of my sister Carolyn, who taught me what never quitting is really all about.

To access audio visit:
www.halleonard.com/mylibrary

Enter Code
5503-5341-3827-5158

ISBN 978-1-57424-348-2
SAN 683-8022

I0792512

Cover by James Creative Group

CENTERSTREAM®

P.O. Box 17878 - Anaheim Hills, CA 92817

www.centerstream-usa.com | centerstrm@aol.com

WSM GRAND OLE OPRY GOSPEL CONCERT

Direct From World Famous Grand Ole Opry

Jim & Jesse and the Virginia Boys
NASHVILLE, TENNESSEE

Mike Stevens
WORLD'S GREATEST HARMONICA PLAYER

The Lewis Family
America's First Family of Gospel Bluegrass
FROM LINCOLNTON, GEORGIA

Bluegrass Mountaineers

BELLEVUE JUNIOR HIGH SCHOOL

CORNER 269 NORTH and NORTH STREET - BELLEVUE, 13 West of Norwalk on Route 20

SAT.-APRIL 9

7:00 P. M.

Spon. By First United Methodist Men

FOR INFORMATION CALL JOHN GIBSON (419) 483-7026

ADM.–$8.00 ADVANCE - $10.00 AT DOOR
CHILDREN 6 to 12 $4.00 ADVANCE, $5.00 AT DOOR – UNDER 6 FREE

For Tickets Send Self-Addressed & Stamped Envelope to:
Mr. & Mrs. John Gibson, P. O. Box 154, Bellevue, OH 44811

Table Of Contents

Introduction

Mike Stevens and Roy Acuff.

Well, let me tell you a bit about myself. First of all, why harp in bluegrass? Well, I was an Ironman Tri-athelete who trained 2 years for the big one in Hawaii, and then one month before the competition, I tore a ligament in my ankle and discovered a stress fracture in my right leg. Anyhow, I had these huge lungs and no where to go, thus my instrument the pneumatic fiddle or harp. I played in several bluegrass bands in Canada. Eventually, I played in a band that was awarded "The Most Promising New Bluegrass Band" at the Central Canadian Bluegrass Awards. This lead to playing on the bill with major American acts, at several Canadian bluegrass festivals. The first group to take me out on a road trip was The Lost and Found from Virginia. Later that year, the Lewis Family started inviting me to bluegrass shows they were playing. Those first shows were very interesting. They would call me up out of the audience to play for very traditional bluegrass audiences, and then they would pass the hat to cover my expenses. Many times we would drive through several states all night long between gigs to play this way. It was very exciting. Almost all of the shows I played this way booked me back the following year with a contract. At one of these shows, Little Roy Lewis introduced me to bluegrass legends Jim & Jesse. They heard me play and then brought me out on their show. After the performance, Jim & Jesse approached me about guesting with them at The Grand Ole Opry. I couldn't believe it! When the day arrived I was a bundle of nerves. The host of the show would be the legendary Roy Acuff. We played The Orange Blossom Special and received a standing ovation, then everything really started rolling. I recorded an album entitled Mike Stevens "Harmonica" - this recording won Bluegrass Recording of the Year at the Central Canadian Bluegrass Awards. It also received very heavy airplay worldwide in the bluegrass world. "Not bad for a harp record!". At the time of this writing, I have played The Grand Ole Opry over 200 times.

My second recording "Blowin Up A Storm" was released by a bluegrass music label called Pinecastle. That record was awarded the top selling recording of the year. "Not bad for a harmonica recording," on a totally bluegrass label.

I have been fortunate enough to play from Japan to Mexico and do many sessions with the style of playing I have developed.

It is not without its drawbacks. I have played so hard that I have pushed my intestines through my stomach wall 5 times. I am currently sewed up with 7 rows of stainless steel wire from my hip to my groin. I guess I'm steel belted now.

I've been fortunate enough to have been awarded Central Canadian Bluegrass Entertainer of the Year 5 years in a row, and as I've said, my first record was awarded Bluegrass Recording of the year. Why I'm telling you this is because I believe this style of playing really works and the possibilities are truly endless. I have given you everything you will need to play my way in this book.

Study, Practice, and Blow man Blow!

Notes On The C Harp

This diagram shows the notes that are available on the diatonic harmonica. The diatonic harp has over three chromatic octaves. This example uses a C harp.

The typical 10 hole harmonica in the key of C:

										B^b ↑ (−2)
	OB=E^b			OB=E^b	OB=G^b	OB=B^b		E^b ↑ (−1)	G^b ↑ (−1)	B ↑ (−1)
BLOW	C ↑	E ↑	G ↑	C ↑	E ↑	G ↑	C ↑	E ↑	G ↑	C ↑
	Hole 1	**Hole 2**	**Hole 3**	**Hole 4**	**Hole 5**	**Hole 6**	**Hole 7**	**Hole 8**	**Hole 9**	**Hole 10**
DRAW	D ↓	G ↓	B ↓	D ↓	F ↓	A ↓	B ↓	D ↓	F ↓	A ↓
	D^b ↓ (−1)	G^b ↓ (−1)	B^b ↓ (−1)	D^b ↓ (−1)		A^b ↓ (−1)	OD=$C^\#$		OD=A^b	OD=$C^\#$
		F ↓ (−2)	A ↓ (−2)							
			A^b ↓ (−3)							

Use this diagram when listening to the beginning of the disc describing the notes that are available on the harmonica.

OB = OVERBLOW
BL = BLOW
DR = DRAW
OD = OVERDRAW

↑ - Blow note.

↑ (−1) - Blow note, bent down one semitone.

↑ (−2) - Blow note, bent down two semitones.

↓ - Draw note.

↓ (−1) - Draw note, bent down one semitone.

↓ (−2) - Draw note, bent down two semitones.

↓ (−3) - Draw note, bent down three semitones.

Learning all of these notes in their order chromatically is extremely helpful in developing originality in your playing. Since you are really painting a picture with your solos why not have all the colors available to paint with.

Remember once you can do all of the techniques necessary, play your scale from bottom to top and top to bottom.

How To Hold The Harp

I really feel the best way for you to hold the harp is whatever feels good and whatever is the most natural for you.

Just keep in mind that you can shape the tone and create some great effects by cupping your hands around the back of the harp.

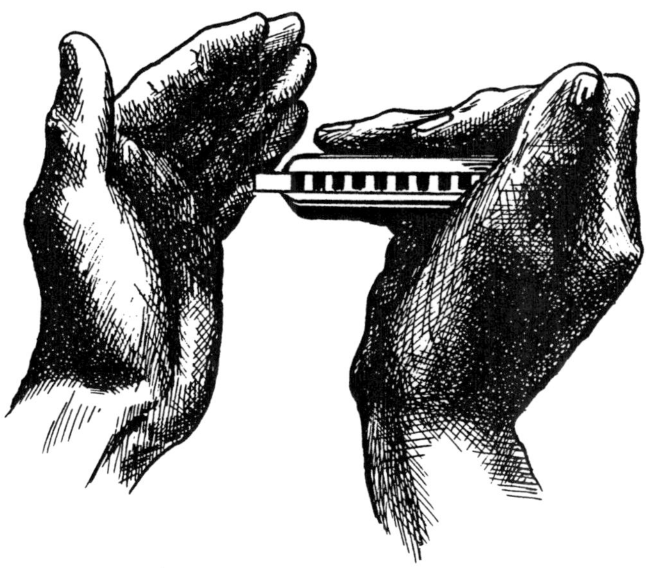

Lip Pursing Method

This is the style I use. The best way to describe it is to pucker up like a kiss and put the harp to your lips. Remember to narrow or tighten your mouth so that just one hole sounds as you breathe in or blow out. Practice this until you can play single notes cleanly. Work on patterns of notes. First start at the low end and play each note blowing in then drawing out all the way up and down the harp. If you are having trouble try taping off every other hole on the harp with scotch tape. Do the exercises described above. As you get used to single notes, take off some tape and try it again. If you get bored, play with your favorite recordings to practice.

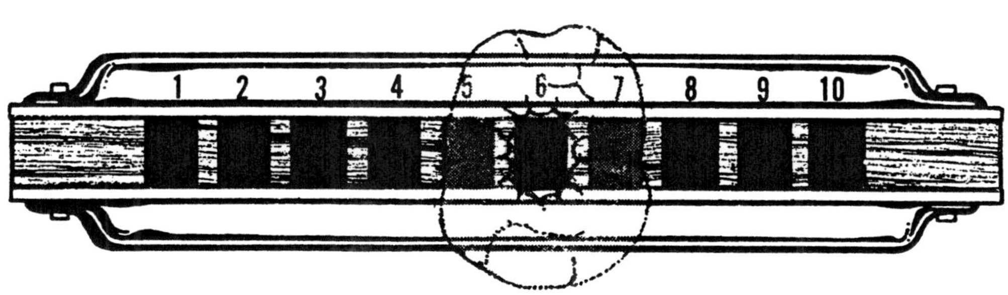

Tongue Blocking Method

I also use this technique in bluegrass, but not as much as lip pursing.

Tongue blocking involves using your tongue to block out certain holes on the harp while you play and playing the notes on either side of your tongue.

You really need to learn both methods, but focus on the lip pursing for playing bluegrass.

If you wish, use the same exercises as you would for the lip pursing method.

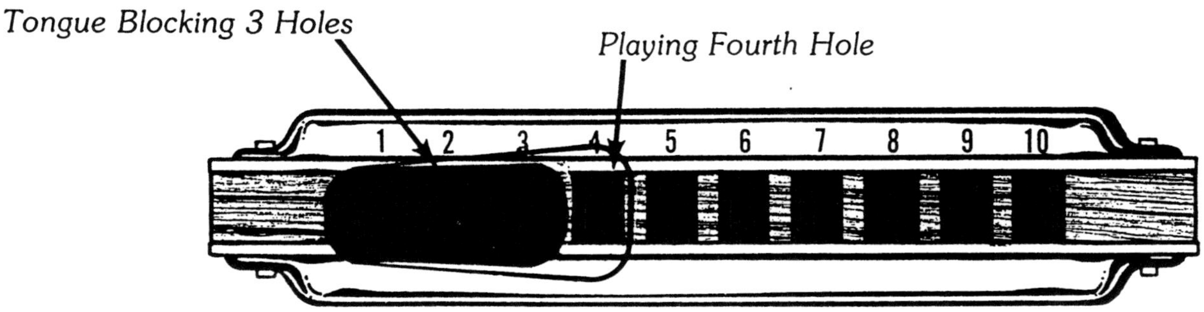

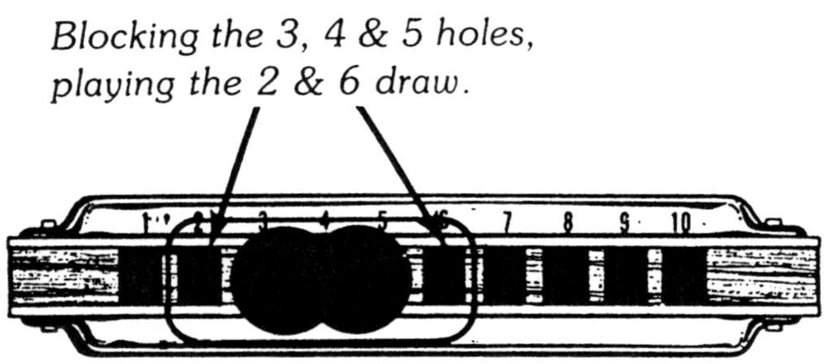

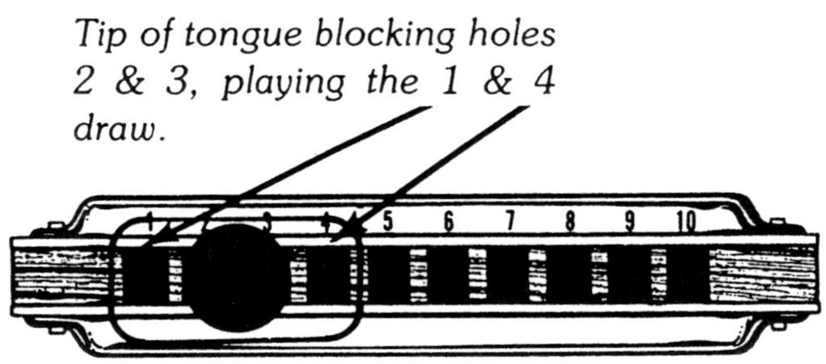

Final Thoughts On Single Notes

You need to develop a feel so that when you take the harp from your hand to your mouth, you can automatically play a single note. I guess it is a muscle memory developed from practice.

Once you can hit single notes, use rhythmic patterns to practice them as in DA DA DA.

Think in terms of a banjo roll or a mandolin picking. It doesn't matter if the notes make sense at this point. Just try to make it rhythmic, then speed it up.

Draw Bending

You must learn this technique in order to play bluegrass my way. It will help you to really wail on tunes and also make the harp more vocal sounding. Also you can play very liquid fiddle runs this way.

This is kind of like learning to ride a bike. It will take you some work to learn, but once you get it, it will be as natural as breathing. Extremely important!

Let's use the 4 draw on a C harp for this remember to have the CD cued up to the right spot to hear what the bend sounds like.

Draw in on the hole number 4. As you are breathing in, make the inside cavity of your mouth bigger. Drop your jaw down and move your tongue to the floor of your mouth. This will make the cavity bigger.

Remember to say AAH while you are breathing in, then when you try to bend the note say OOOOH and increase the pressure you are breathing in with. Think about making the sound drop in pitch.

Really concentrate on the sound of the straight draw and how it changes with the bend.

Remember -- AAAAAAAAH

OOOOOOH

At first your bends will be completely uncontrolled, but that's okay. Just keep bending.

Now that you can bend a note the work starts. I compare this stage to someone learning the fiddle. On the fiddle you have no frets to show you the hand position required for certain notes. So, you practice your intonation to make your notes the proper pitch. It is a lot of work.

The harp is no different, now that you can bend a note you have to learn to bend the note the proper amount to produce a note that is the correct pitch.

If you have access to a keyboard even a cheap one, it will come in handy as you can play the note on the keyboard then play the note on the harp to check your pitch on the bends. Remember all the notes are there, white and black keys just refer to the chart at the beginning of the book.

Get a cheap piano book that tells you what notes the keys are. Take the notes that are in your harp and put them on the piano keys.

On the draw 1 you can drop the pitch of the D note to a Db /C#.

On the draw 2 you can drop the pitch of the G, 2 semi-tones. First to a Gb then, further to an F.

On the draw 3 you can drop the pitch of the B, 3 semi-tones. First to a Bb then to an A and finally to an Ab.

On the draw 4 you can drop the pitch of the D, 1 semi-tone to a Db/C#.

On the draw 6 you can drop the pitch of the A, 1 semi-tone to an Ab.

When you are practicing these bends, don't always bend down to them. Sometimes you should start on a bend and go up or down, or go from a bent note to a bent note on another hole.

Blow Bends

The blow bends will help you play some really dynamic runs in the high end of the harp. This is an area that too many harp players ignore because it is a little tough, really it's not any harder just different.

We will try the 10 hole blow for this. First you will have to be able to play this note cleanly blowing out. While you are blowing out, tighten your embouchure and bring your tongue up towards the roof of your mouth and increase your pressure. Focus the air on the reed, really direct the air pressure down on the reed and keep your lips tight as in a fish imitation.

Really focus on dropping the pitch of the note. My tongue is in a U shape when I am directing this air pressure on the reed.

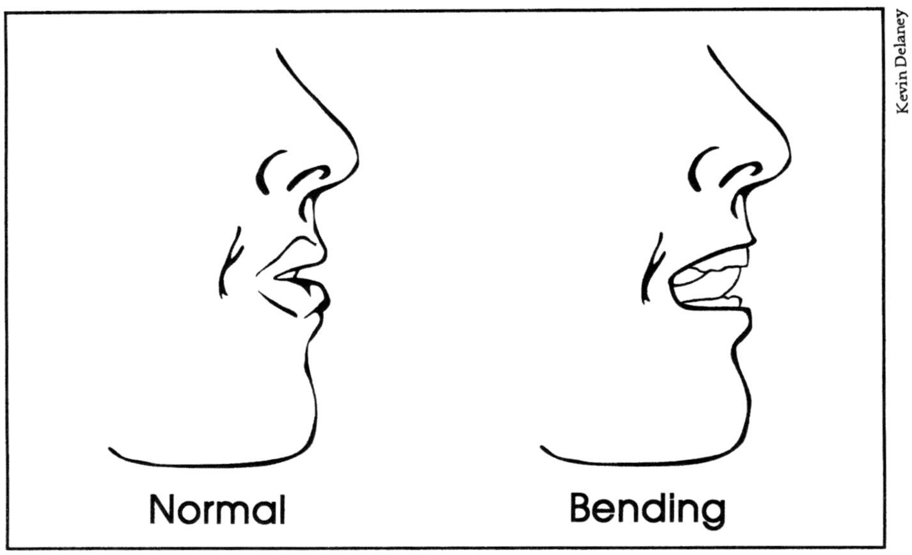

You will need to develop specific muscles in your embouchure to do these bends your mouth might ache a little bit. Don't worry that's a good thing like when you're lifting weights you are a little stiff the next day, no big deal, just keep at it. Working on blow bends will improve the sound of all your single note blow playing by strengthening up these muscles. Also it will set up your next lesson when you need to learn overblowing. Remember to try the same exercises as I have suggested for draw bends they are just as important.

Blow bending -- Key of C Harp

On the blow 8, you can drop the pitch of the E, one semi-tone to an Eb.

On the blow 9, you can drop the pitch of the G, one semi-tone to a Gb.

On the blow 10, you can drop the pitch of the C, two semi-tones to a B and then to a Bb.

Overblowing

This technique, along with overdrawing, will enable you to play the so called missing notes that makes your harmonica a completely chromatic instrument. It is a little tough to learn at first but I have a method of getting them easier.

First of all, about the easiest harp to play them on are the Golden Melodies. Although any diatonic will overblow and overdraw.

You should use an OLD harp for this part. Preferably in the key of C. You will need to be able to remove the cover plates.

What you need to do at this point is to set the reed gaps on hole 6. What you will notice if you set the reed gaps very close to the reed plate the harp will not be as responsive, and if you push it too close to the plate it will not play at all. What I am looking for here is to set your reed gap as close as you can while letting the reed still play with light air pressure.

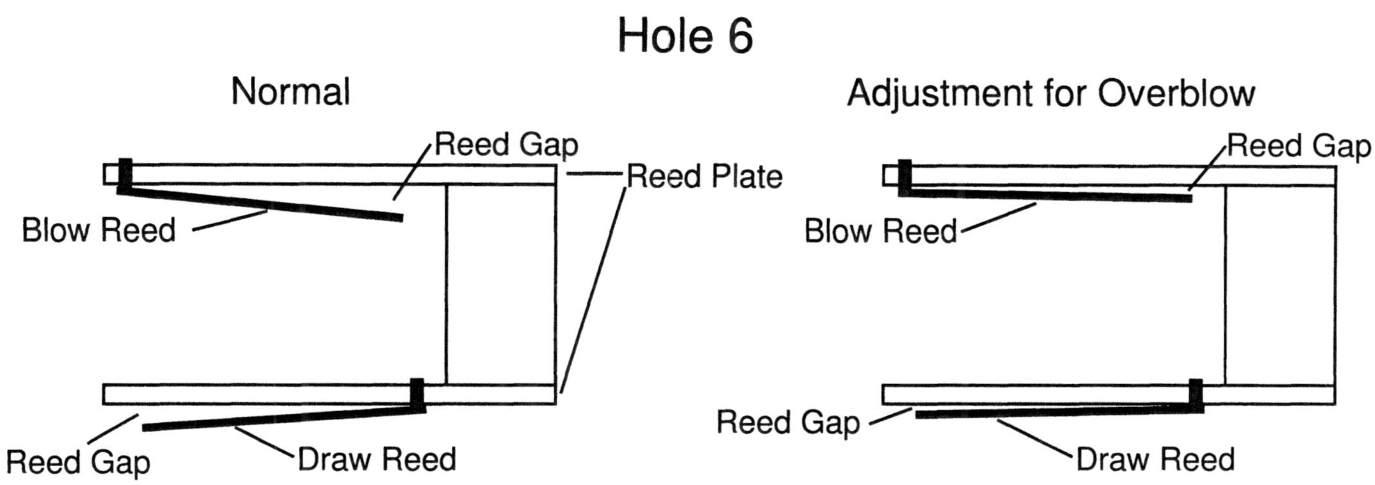

It is not necessary to do this to learn how to overblow, however I have found you will be able to get one quicker using this method.

Okay, now cue up the CD to the correct spot.

Blow on the hole 6 and shape you mouth like you were going to do a blow bend. Really tighten up your jaw and your mouth. Think about pushing the blow reed down with the air pressure. Make the reed crack or distort. Listen to the CD to hear what that sounds like. The reed will go silent and make like a feedback hissing noise before it cracks in. You will definitely wreck some harps learning this technique because in the beginning a person tends to use too much air pressure on the overblow, but once you have learned how to do this, you can control them with light air pressure, and even bend them like a draw note.

Once you can play the overblow easily you can make the gaps on your reeds a little larger, just so the harp will be a little more responsive .

The hole 4, 5 and 6 will overblow in the way I have described, however, the hole 1 overblow is a different technique.

The hole 1 overblow is hard to sustain. I use it more as a passing note in a phrase. To get the 1 overblow, you must start on the draw 1, breathing in then play the blow 1. The vibration of the draw 1 sets up the hole 1 overblow and makes it easier. If you were blowing out a candle just using the air in you mouth, not your lungs, this is the same technique. It is like a quick blast of air. Try making like a Whhhhht sound with just the air in your mouth. It is a tough one but it is useful.

Overblowing notes on a C harp.

On the overblow 1, you will get the missing Eb between hole 1 and hole 2.

On the overblow 4, you will get the missing Eb between hole 4 and hole 5.

On the overblow 5, you will get the missing F# between hole 5 and hole 6.

On the overblow 6, you will get the missing Bb between hole 6 and hole 7.

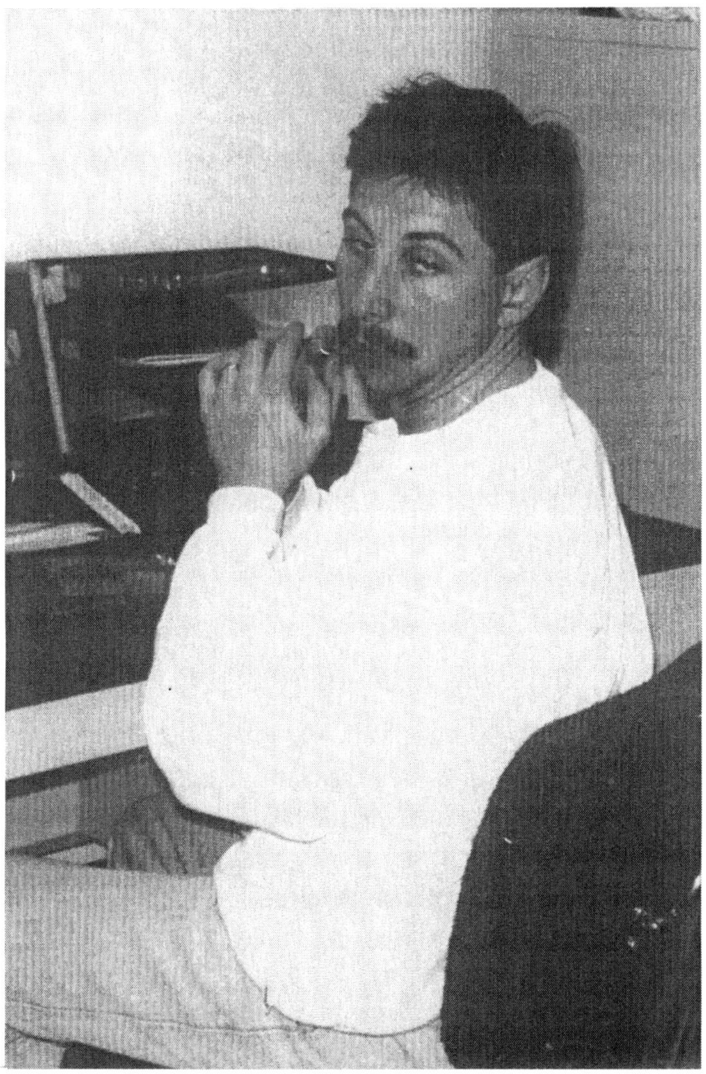

After you have tuned your harp for eight hours, this will happen to you.

Overdrawing

This technique is kind of like an overblow in reverse, since you are using a draw note and raising it in pitch. To play a chromatic scale you will need to overdraw the hole 7 and the hole 9.

Again, set your reed gaps very close on these two holes. It will make the overdraws a little easier.

Draw in on the hole 7, while you are drawing in, tighten up you mouth and jaw and really increase the vacuum you are creating on the hole. This takes quite a lot of pressure and a very tight seal on the harp to do this. The note will crack up just like an overblow. All I can say is just keep trying and you will get it.

Key of C harp.

On the overdraw 7, you will get the missing C# from hole 7 to hole 8.

On the overdraw 9, you will get the missing G# from hole 9 to hole 10.

On the overdraw 10, you will get an additional C# on top of the C.

Vibrato

Vibrato will give your playing a richness that will make it sound more full and more vocal sounding.

There are several types of vibrato. The one I use the most is a throat glottis vibrato. It will involve you controlling the slap of your glottis down in your throat and really opening up your stomach and chest cavity. This will let the tone resonate and with the glottis slapping will create a rich controlled tone.

Try blowing out saying UH UH UH UH way down in your throat. Now try breathing in saying the same thing. Now try it with your harp and try to control it. Remember to listen to the CD for examples.

Another type of vibrato is created with your tongue wagging while you are playing. It is a gentler vibrato and not as rich as a glottis vibrato.

Also you can create a vibrato with your mouth opening and closing slightly on the harp, while you are playing a note. This vibrato is very useful on blow bends and overblows.

There is another type of vibrato that can be created by opening and closing your hands around the harp while you are playing.

Attacking The Notes

The way I attack the notes has a lot to do with the driving sound I get on the harp.

Make sure you have the disc cued up to this technique for examples.

Draw in on hole 3 and say DAT DAT DAT DAT. Listen for the hard edge it produces on the note.

Now try it saying OOOH OOOH OOOH. You can really notice a difference it will be a smoother sound.

Just remember to be aware of your annunciation and try different words or parts of words while playing.

Maybe even take something your reading and try reading it through the harp. Think of how different the banjo sounds from the fiddle and approach your phrasing from different points of view. Hard edged or smooth, it is not just the amount of pressure you hit the note with that makes it punch. it is also the way you enunciate.

Banjo Patterns

This is a very important part of my style of playing. My approach to a solo is to try and make the break I am playing really cook rhythm wise. Even if you can't play intricate patterns on your solo you can mess with the timing to make it very interesting and unique.

Try really listening to the mandolin's chop and try to slowly work out a simple phrase that will fit rhythmically with the mandolin chop. Once you have a simple pattern worked out, start to add things to it that will lend it more to the melody or the feel of the tune, but don't add anything that detracts from the feel of it. For me, feel is the whole thing.

If you do this, you will find you will start to create your own patterns or rolls that you can build on for all types of tunes and all styles of music.

A lot of my patterns that I created early on for bluegrass harp playing are on the CD and tabbed out in the book. Try them, learn them and create your own. It's really rewarding.

A hint:

A lot of simple blues licks will work well rhythmically to start to build your rolls.

Wind Chops Or Bluegrass Chugging

As you listen to bluegrass pay attention to the structure of the music. Listen for what instrument is playing at a give time. You will notice this especially true when someone is soloing. Try not to listen to the soloist but listen to what's going on from the support players. Now concentrate on the mandolin and try to emulate the mandolin chop with your harp. There are several examples that I use on the CD.

Again, I keep stressing this, but it's important. "Timing is very important." Don't worry about your chord position right now, just try to make the harp add something to the rhythm section.

You may want to check out Sonny Terry, for some really cool chugging patterns that can be adapted to wind chops.

Some Types of Chops

Breathing in say -- BUC AH, then blow out one breathe. Try to speed it up and make it rhythmic. Listen to the CD.

Try a straight BUC BUC BUC while breathing in. Remember to really get a tight seal on the harp and then almost pull the harp away from your lips to make a really abrupt cut off on the chop.

Another chop involves what's called a tongue block octave.

What I want you to do is to put your tongue in the center of the harp and play notes on both sides of your tongue at the same time.

Listen to what it sounds like on the disc. You will eventually play notes' octaves apart because your tongue blocks off the middle part of the octave and you play part of the lower octave and part of the higher octave at the same time.

Work on moving this all around the harp to get pleasing sounds. Now you can also do a wind chop using this. It is like a regular wind chop except that at the beginning or the Buc part of the BUC AH you are doing a tongue block octave.

Try it, see what you think.

Train Rhythm

The train whistle is a bent chord on the draw 2, 3, and 4. Say WAH while you are breathing in and opening and closing your hands around the harp for effect.

Now to get the train moving, you have to say TUCATA breathing in and give a breath out after it. Listen to the CD and slowly speed up your pattern until your train is rolling down the rails.

Tuning Your Harps

This is pretty important if you really want your harps to sound good, and it could possibly save you a few bucks on harps.

What you will need is a small piece of brass or any metal that is really thin, that will fit under the reeds. Any hobby shop should have something. Also, you will need a very small file. Again, the hobby shop will have a selection of cheap files. Just find one that feels the best. Personally for this step, I use a little Dremel tool and I get some dental bits from a dentist. I adjust the dental bits to fit into the Dremel for filing my reeds. You will also need a chromatic tuner with a mic input . The one I'm using now is a Sabine ST-1500 autotuner. It's relatively cheap and it works good for tuning the harp.

You will also need a small set of screwdrivers.

I have included a chart of all the notes blowing and drawing for all keys of diatonic harps.

Here's what I do when I tune:

First, I will make a chart or picture of the harp. Let's say I'm tuning a C harp, here's what my chart might look like.

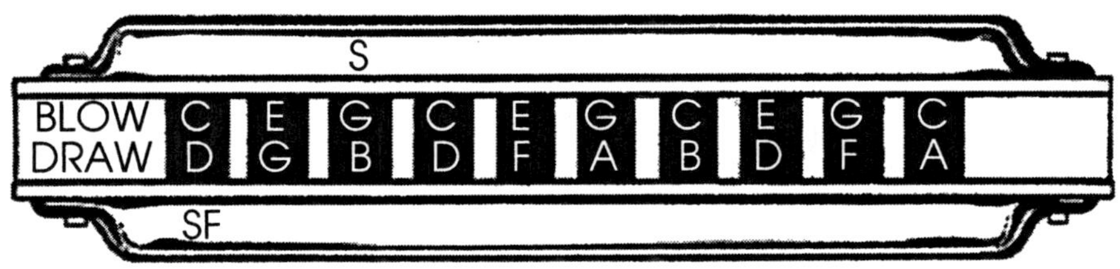

Now, I will play all of the notes into the tuner and mark the notes that are flat or sharp. let's say the 1 draw is slightly flat. I will make a small SF on the chart. Now the 3 blow was sharp. I will make that with a small S. After I have checked out the whole harp, and I have my chart filled out, I will go back and start my tuning.

I will remove the cover plates on the harp and I will slip a thin piece of brass or a thin piece of metal, such as a single edged razor, under the draw 1 reed. That reed is slightly flat so I must raise the pitch of the reed slightly. To do this I will gently file a little weight off the tip of the reed.

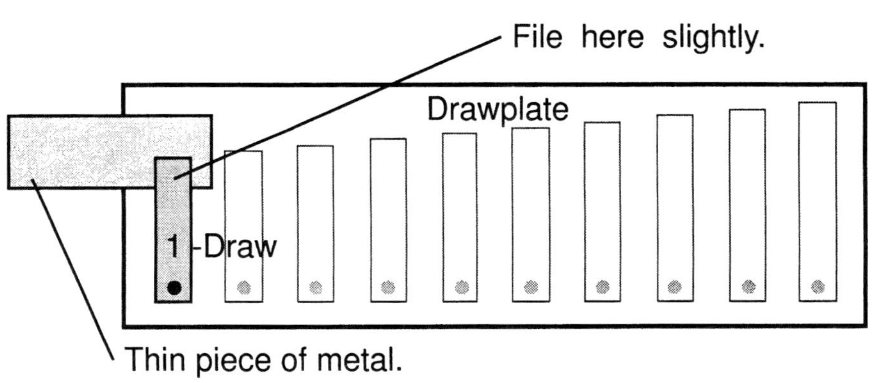

Now put the plates back on the harp and play that note into your tuner and see where you are at.

Now for that 3 blow that is a little sharp. Take off your cover plates and if you can take off your reed plates (if they are screwed together). If they are not, you must take your small screwdriver and push the reed up through the slit in the reed plate. Slip the thin piece of metal under the tip of the reed.

To make the reed go down in pitch, you must scratch along the base of the reed where it is connected to the plate.

Once you have filed your reed, put the harp back together and play the note into the tuner and see where you're at.

This process takes a lot of patience and you will destroy a lot of harps learning the process, but anything good is worth the effort. Good Luck!!

My harps are not tuned to 440, they are probably about 442 - 444. Remember that when you are playing the note into the tuner, don't bend it or play it too hard. Just a natural breath will do it. Also, for some reason the pitch of reeds continue to rise a little after you tune them, so easy does it.

Natural Minor

You can buy harps that are tuned to a natural minor already. They allow you to play minor scales in second position and get some really nice chords. Lee Osker makes some really good harps in this tuning, but if you would like you can tune your own this way.

D Harp

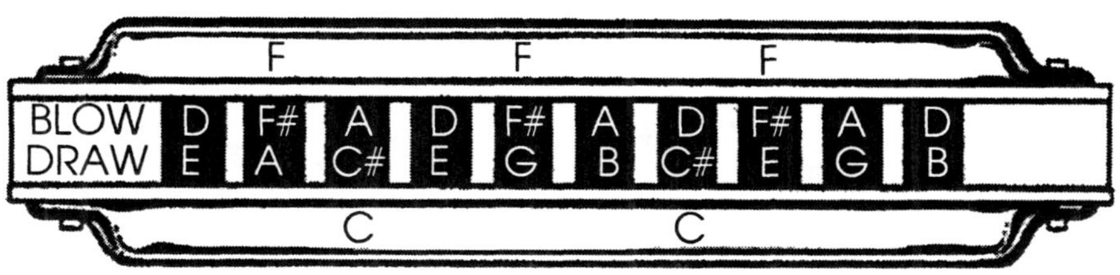

What I do is I drop the pitch of the blow 2, blow 5 and blow 8, one semi-tone, then the draw 3 and draw 7 one semi-tone. This will let you play a D harp in the key of Am in second position.

There are two ways to drop the pitch of the reed. One we talked about, (the filing at the base). The other way is by dropping a small piece of solder on the free end of the reed, increasing its' weight and dropping its pitch, then just file and tune as necessary.

This technique is used on any harp in any key.

Remember try it on an old harp first!

The following illustrations give you a note layout of all keys of harps:

Key of G

	1	2	3	4	5	6	7	8	9	10
BLOW	G	B	D	G	B	D	G	B	D	G
DRAW	A	D	F#	A	C	E	F#	A	C	E

Key of Db

	1	2	3	4	5	6	7	8	9	10
BLOW	Db	F	Ab	Db	F	Ab	Db	F	Ab	Db
DRAW	Eb	Ab	C	Eb	Gb	Bb	C	Eb	Gb	Bb

Key of Ab

	1	2	3	4	5	6	7	8	9	10
BLOW	Ab	C	Eb	Ab	C	Eb	Ab	C	Eb	Ab
DRAW	Bb	Eb	G	Bb	Db	F	G	Bb	Db	F

Key of D

	1	2	3	4	5	6	7	8	9	10
BLOW	D	F#	A	D	F#	A	D	F#	A	D
DRAW	E	A	C#	E	G	B	C#	E	G	B

Key of A

	1	2	3	4	5	6	7	8	9	10
BLOW	A	C#	E	A	C#	E	A	C#	E	A
DRAW	B	E	G#	B	D	F#	G#	B	D	F#

Key of Eb

	1	2	3	4	5	6	7	8	9	10
BLOW	Eb	G	Bb	Eb	G	Bb	Eb	G	Bb	Eb
DRAW	F	Bb	D	F	Ab	C	D	F	Ab	C

Key of Bb

	1	2	3	4	5	6	7	8	9	10
BLOW	Bb	D	F	Bb	D	F	Bb	D	F	Bb
DRAW	C	F	A	C	Eb	G	A	C	Eb	G

Key of E

	1	2	3	4	5	6	7	8	9	10
BLOW	E	G#	B	E	G#	B	E	G#	B	E
DRAW	F#	B	D#	F#	A	C#	D#	F#	A	C#

Key of B

	1	2	3	4	5	6	7	8	9	10
BLOW	B	D#	F#	B	D#	F#	B	D#	F#	B
DRAW	C#	F#	A#	C#	E	G#	A#	C#	F	G#

Key of F

	1	2	3	4	5	6	7	8	9	10
BLOW	F	A	C	F	A	C	F	A	C	F
DRAW	G	C	E	G	Bb	D	E	G	Bb	D

Key of C

	1	2	3	4	5	6	7	8	9	10
BLOW	C	E	G	C	E	G	C	E	G	C
DRAW	D	G	B	D	F	A	B	D	F	A

Key of F#

	1	2	3	4	5	6	7	8	9	10
BLOW	F#	A#	C#	F#	A#	C#	F#	A#	C#	F#
DRAW	G#	C#	E#	G#	B	D#	E#	G#	B	D#

Harp Positions Theory

Well, I really hate to get into music theory because I don't know that much about it. However the best way that I have seen to describe harmonica positions included the circle of fifths chart.

Please take the time to figure this out, it will help you immensely. If you do, you will eventually internalize it and it will be easy.

To figure out what harp to use you will need to know the key that the song is in. The key is really the most important note of the song. In bluegrass, usually the last note of the song, lets say it is a G if it is followed by a G chord will mean that the song will be in the key of G. This would mean the tonic would be G.

There is an easy method to find out what the other chords usually are. It is the circle of fifths chart. Here it is, take a look at it.

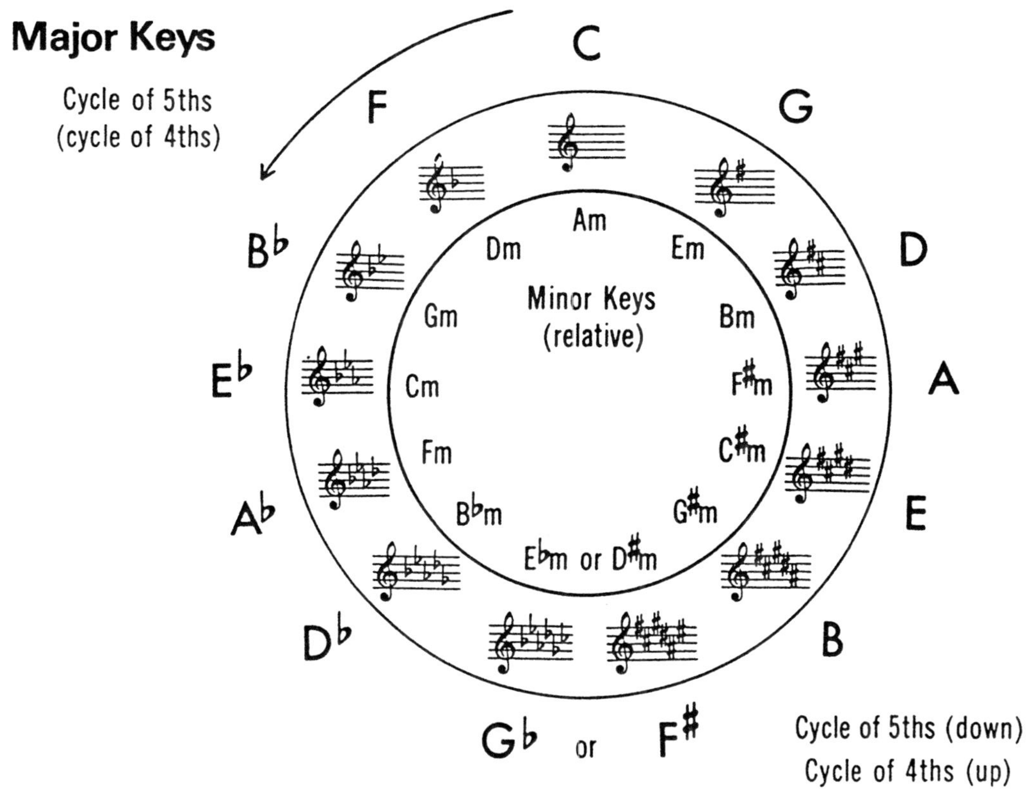

Now that you know the tonic, or the key of the song, lets say it is G. If you move one step clockwise on the chart, you will find D. D is the dominant chord to the tonic G.

If you move one step counterclockwise from G you will find C. C is the subdominant cord in the key of G. This means that if your song is in the key of G, most likely your chords will be G, C, D.

This chart works for any standard tunes. Just find out what key your tune is in, move one set clockwise and one step counterclockwise and you will have the 3 chords in your tune.

The same circle of fifths will tell you all of your harmonica positions easily and will tell you your options on what keys of harps to play for which songs.

You can say all the notes on the circle are keys of songs and when you move one step counterclockwise from any key, that will be the harp you would use in second position. Two steps counterclockwise would be the harp for 3rd position, 3 steps - 4th position, 4 steps back - 5th position. This will tell you what harp to use all the way up to 12th position. This is the easiest way for me to understand it.

The most important positions to look at initially are 1st and 2nd. A lot of what I do is in 2nd position, or cross harp. However, I also play in the other positions, and find them very useful. Here are the main ones to fool with.

1st position - Key of C on a C harp
2nd position - Key of G on a C harp
3rd position - Key of D on a C harp
4th position - Key of A on a C harp
5th position - Key of E on a C harp
6th position - Key of B on a C harp
11th position - Key of B on a C harp
12th position - Key of F on a C harp

Check out the circle of fifths chart when looking at this. 3rd and 4th positions are very nice for playing a lot of minor keyed tunes. Just experiment with all the positions and see what you think.

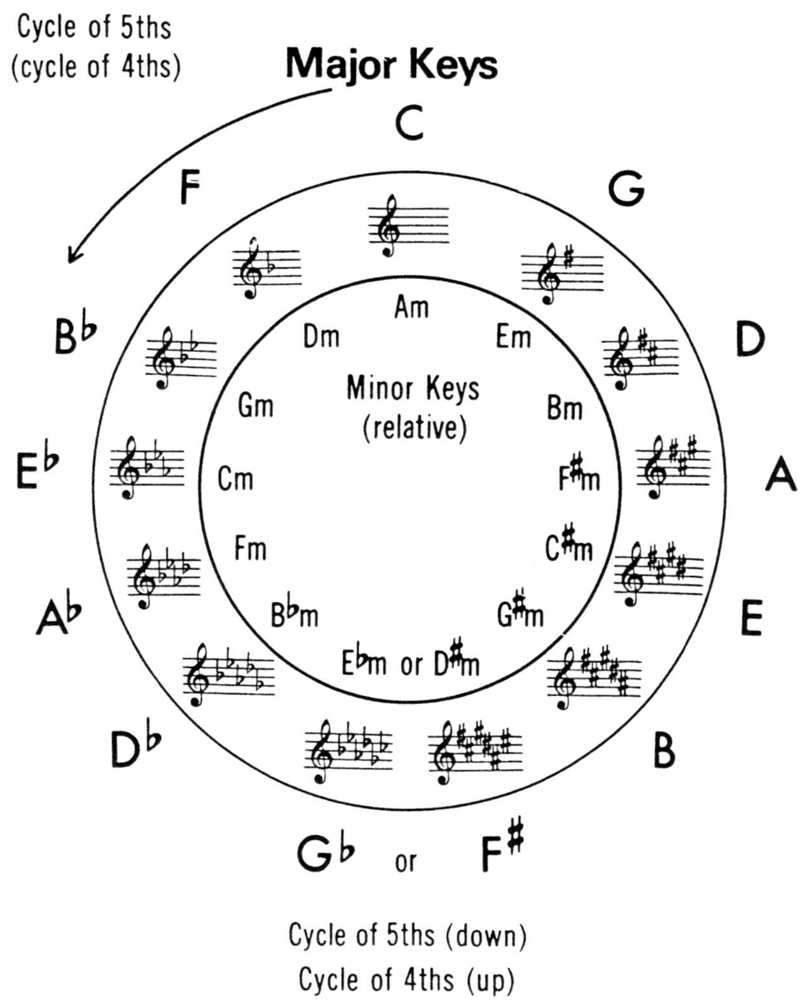

Playing Live On A Sound System

The way I think bluegrass harp sounds the best is acoustically. What this means is I use a vocal mic on a stand and I play back off the mic far enough that I can shape the sounds with my cupped hands.

Basically I have the gain on the mic set about the same as if I was going to sing through it. If you get too close to the mic, the tone of the harp changes a great deal, and does not sound natural. It will have a more electric sound. Fine for some styles of music, but not great for bluegrass.

You will find patience a valuable charàcter trait here, since harp in bluegrass is very new and most sound guys in bluegrass don't know how to treat it. A lot of them are used to country players who cup the mic and play more electric style. You will just have to stay on it and get the sound you want.

As a hint, here is what you can do if you don't have enough in the mains, or monitors and have asked already to have it increased. Just play softer and back up a little from the mic. When people start complaining that they can't hear the harp, the sound guy will usually increase it a bit. Kind of a dirty trick, but it has come in handy.

Just work for the most natural sound you can get.

Photo: Ronald L. Stuckey

Mike Stevens with Jim and Jesse and the Virginia Boys at the Grand Ole Opry.

Writing Music With The Harp

One of the most enjoyable parts of my playing the harp has come from writing tunes on the instrument. Here are some of my ideas on the subject.

Carry a small microcassette recorder with you and record any new licks or ideas you come up with. Sometimes when you string these licks together a strong melody could develop.

I usually find that my best songs sound good with just the harp solo, without other instruments, at least at first.

Playing your ideas solo will really make you concentrate on the timing of the melody and to keep it interesting.

Sometimes my ideas come from very percussive sounds. i.e. I once wrote a tune listening to the rhythm of an exercise bike. You can add melody later.

If you want to try something for inspiration, try turning the sound down on your TV and play along with what you see. Play as if you are providing a sound track. This is helpful as different types of tunes definitely have different feelings attached to them. You might be surprised what you come up with.

Above all else, remember these are your songs and there are no rules. Just go for it.

Bill Monroe and Mike Stevens.

WSM GRAND OLE OPRY
BLUEGRASS &
GOSPEL CONCERT
SUN. - FEB. 2
2:00 P. M.
BILL MONROE and the Bluegrass Boys
Jim & Jesse and the Virginia Boys
ADM.: $8.00 Advance -
$10.00 at door -
CHILDREN 1/2 price
also
Mike
Stevens
Sponsored by
Appomattox
Athletic Booster Club
APPOMATTOX
HIGH SCHOOL AUDITORIUM

Jam Session Etiquette

When you are ready to start playing with other people, or what's called jamming, there are some things you should know.

Here are the most common mistakes players make.

1. Don't just run up to a jam session and start playing. Listen for a while, figure out if the tuning is 440 and if they are playing songs that are at your level.
2. Remember, be polite while you are playing and listen and play quietly trying to make whoever is soloing or singing, sound better.
3. Don't play all the time! Bluegrass is a team sport. Wait you turn, then wail.
4. Make sure your harps are in tune.

Probably the best way to find out where bluegrass is happening is by checking out your local music shop and asking if they know about any bluegrass clubs in the area. Also, find a public radio station and see if they have a bluegrass show. If they do, chances are they will announce upcoming events and jam sessions in your area. Another good way to find out is by going to a bluegrass festival and asking around.

Also try:

Bluegrass Unlimited Magazine
P.O. Box 111
Broad Run, Va
22014

IBMA
207 East Second St.
Owensboro, Ky
42303

Bluegrass Canada Magazine
#1-231 Victoria St.
Kamloops, BC
Canada
V2C 2A1

American Harmonica Newsletter
2362 W. Territorial Rd
Battle Creek, MI
49015-4956

Harmonica World
c/o Norm Dobson
7 Sewall St
Peabody, MASS
01960 -5516

Bluegrass NOW
PO Box 2020
Rolla, MO
65401

SPAH
The Society for the Preservation and Advancement of the Harmonica
P.O. Box 865
Troy, MI
48099-0865

HIP - Harmonica Information Publication
203 Fourteenth Ave
San Francisco, CA
94418-1007

On the Internet, there is a Harmonica List called Harp L, it is terrific.

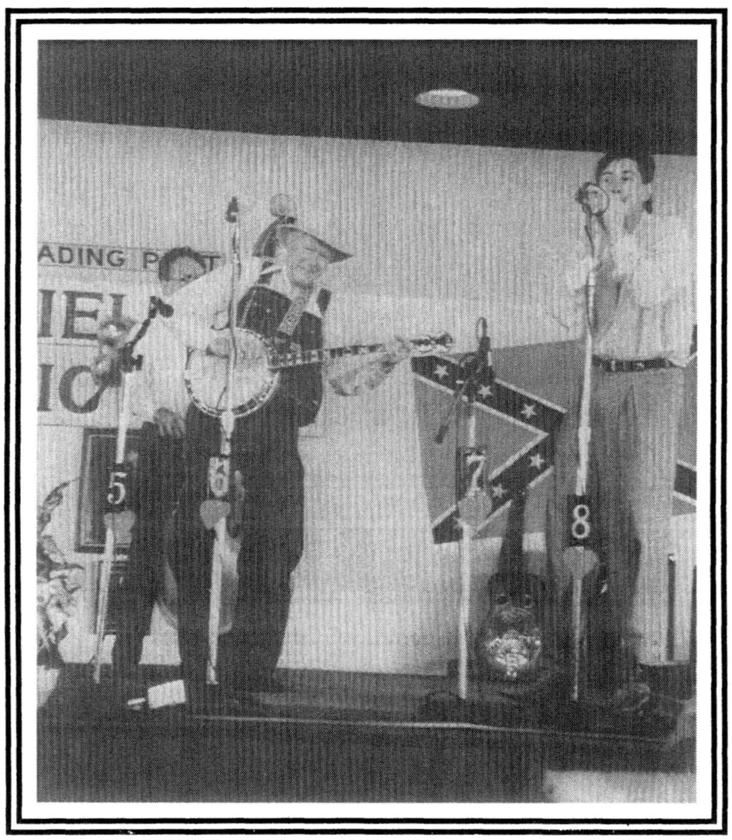

Brother Oswald and Mike Stevens.

Some Thoughts On Playing

I don't know what level you are at reading this, so I will start at the beginning.

The real heart of bluegrass music in my opinion comes from the fact that many of the true inventors and pioneers in this music are still alive and creating music. It is a very new art form, as far as music is concerned and there are many people trying to preserve the traditional sounds of the music. What I am getting at, is that harmonica is not a (Traditional) bluegrass instrument. It is something that I am working at and developing. At the time of this writing, I have been working at bluegrass for 16 years. It has been a difficult but extremely rewarding journey. It has gone from being shunned at bluegrass jam sessions, because I'm playing a toy, all the way to playing over 200 shows with Jim & Jesse at the Grand Ole Opry.

My point is this, "Don't expect to be welcomed with open arms to every bluegrass jam session." You will have to play so good that they can't ignore you. This might mean some frustrating experiences for you, but don't give up.

More and more harp players are being accepted and now at my shows, I'm giving informal seminars to all kinds of harp players breaking into bluegrass.

It's wide open. If you have the determination and love for the music the sky is the limit. Most people who play an instrument in a certain style have copied or learned from somebody popular in that style. An example might be Bill Monroe or Jesse McReynolds for mandolin, or Earl Scruggs for banjo.

With the harp in bluegrass, I had no boundaries since it was a new instrument played this way. There was no one to copy, so my style owes a great deal to the Mississippi Sheiks and Son House, as well as Bill Monroe and Earl Scruggs. In my opinion, Son House and Bill Monroe created the same intensity and honesty in their music.

It is this feeling, that I hope to capture and experience when I play. There is a real power in the music and when it's racing through you, there's no better feeling in the world. My goal is to share that feeling with whoever is listening.

Circa 1925

Amazing Grace

I'm using a C harp on this song. It has some tricky blow bends and some bluesy draw bends. Just remember to check out the CD for an example.

My favorite memory of this song comes from the time I got to play it at the old Ryman Auditorium in Nashville. They had just opened up the old Opry to shoot some TV shows. The Ryman was in its original state, before the 1994 renovations. They had spotlights shining up on the stained glass windows from outside the building. It was a sight I will never forget. What inspiration.

Arrangement by Mike Stevens

C-Part

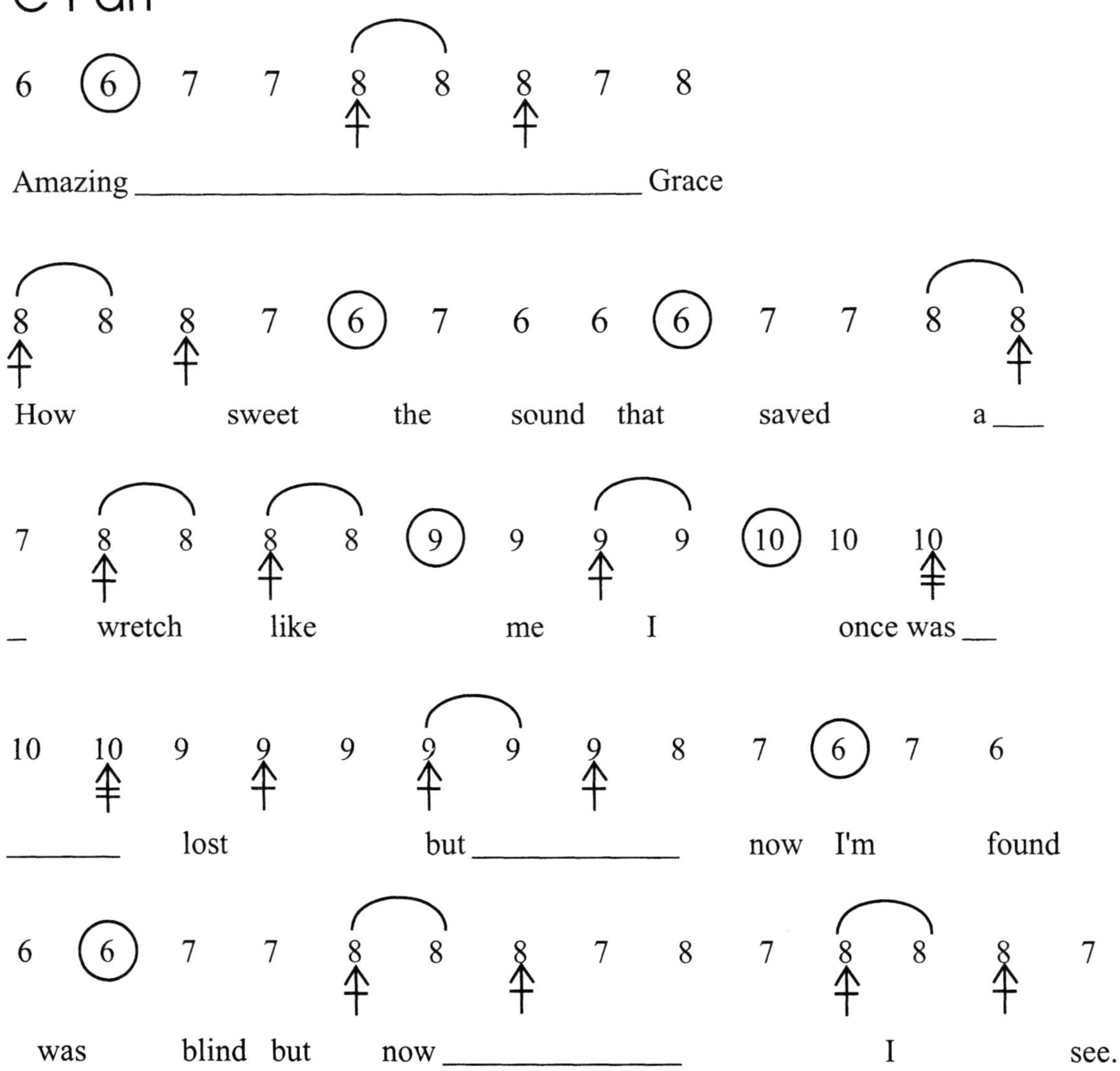

This is the C part of the song or the high notes at the beginning.

C-Harp Beginner

Amazing Grace

Arrangement by Mike Stevens

C-Harp
G-Part

This is the introduction or run down into the G section

④ ④ 4 ③ ② ② ② ② ①

↓ ⇊ ⇊

② ② ③ ③ ② ③ ③ ③ ② 2 ② ①

⇊ ⇊

Amazing________Grace____________ how sweet the sound

① 2 ② ② ③ ③ ② ③ ③ 4 ④

⇊

that saved a wretch like me

③ 4 ④ 4 ③ ③ ② ③ ③ ③ ② 2 ② ①

⇊ ⇊

I once was lost but now I'm found

① 2 ② ② ③ ③ ② ③ ② ③ ③ ②

⇊ ⇊

was blind but now I see.

He's Got The Whole World In His Hands

I'm using a C harp in the key of G.

Remember to hit your bends with the correct pitch and keep this tune really bouncy. Have fun with it

Arrangement by Mike Stevens

C-Harp

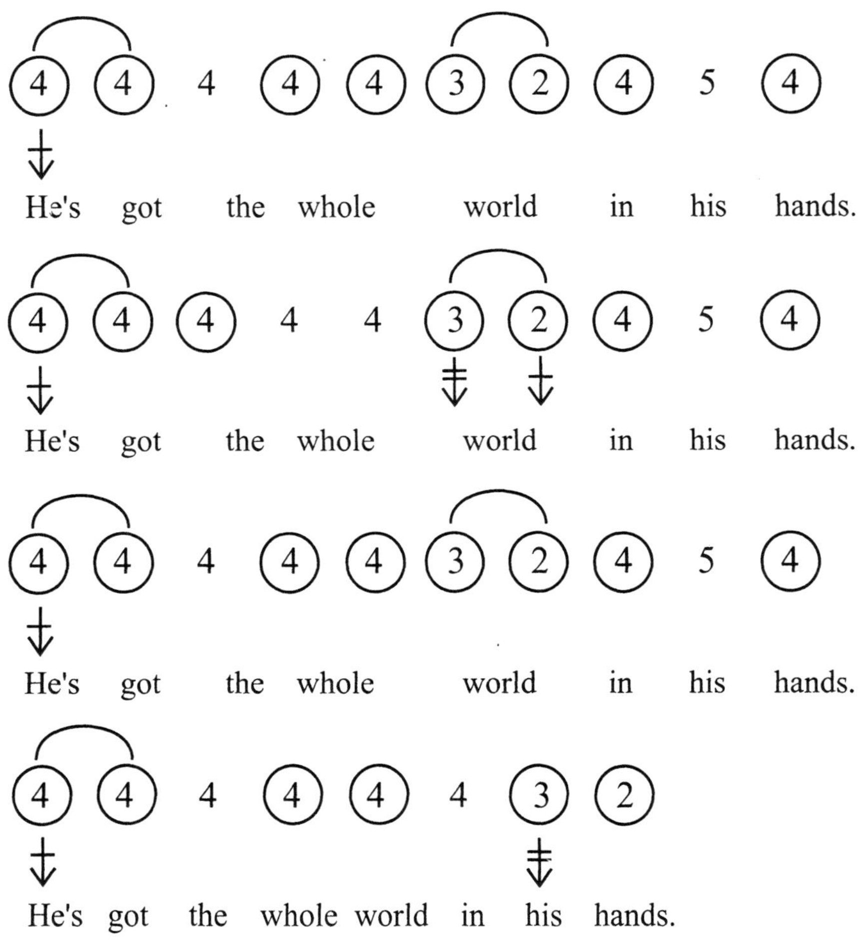

Life's Railway To Heaven

I'm using a 365 Marineband on this tune, but, you can use a normal C harp. Remember to really feel it. It is probably inspired by Sonny Boy Williamson, since I always loved the solo stuff he did.

Think deep tone on this.

Arrangement by Mike Stevens

C-Harp

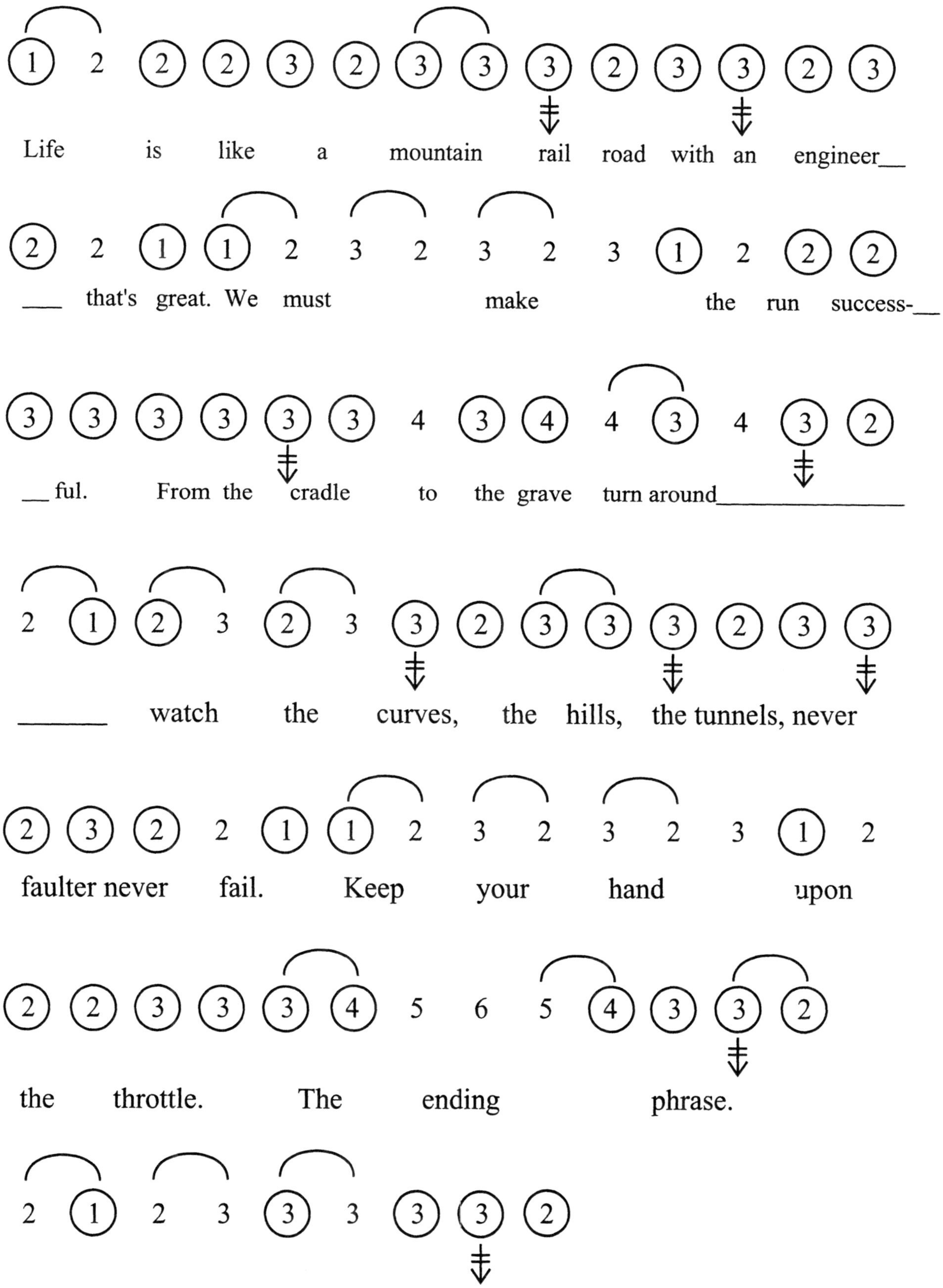

Sweet Hour Of Prayer

I'm using a D harp in the key of A on this tune. It was really tough for me to make that overblow sound sweet on this song. It is really a good introduction to overblowing for you.

Good Luck.

Arrangement by Mike Stevens

D-Harp
Part One

(2) (3) 4 (4) (4) 5 5 OB 6 5 (4) (3) (3)

Sweet hour of prayer sweet hour of prayer that calls me from

(3)↓ (2) (3) 4 (3)↓ (2) (3) 4 (4) (4) 5 5 OB

a world of care and bids me at my fathers

6 5 (4) (3) (3) (3)↓ (2) (3) (3)↓ (2)

throne. Make all my wants and wishes known.

Part Two

(4) 6 5 6 5 (4) (3) (4)

In seasons of distress and grief

(4) 6 5 6 5 (4) (3) (3)↓

my soul has often found relief.

Part Three

(2) (3) 4 (4) (4) 5 5 OB 6

5 (4) (3) (3) (3)↓ (2) (3) (3)↓ 2

My wife and I with our son Colin on his first trip to the Grand Ole Opry.

Bluegrass Connection and me, just before the show, Bluegrass with Class, in Prince Edward Island, Canada.

Me and Jesse McReynolds at the legendary WSM Radio station doing an interview.

Red Haired Boy

This tune is a lot of fun. I'm using a D harp in the key of A. You will really feel a sense of accomplishment when you nail this tune. It will surprise a lot of pickers when you play it. Also, it's a good lesson on how a fiddle tune is put together.

Arrangement by Mike Stevens

Part One
D-Harp

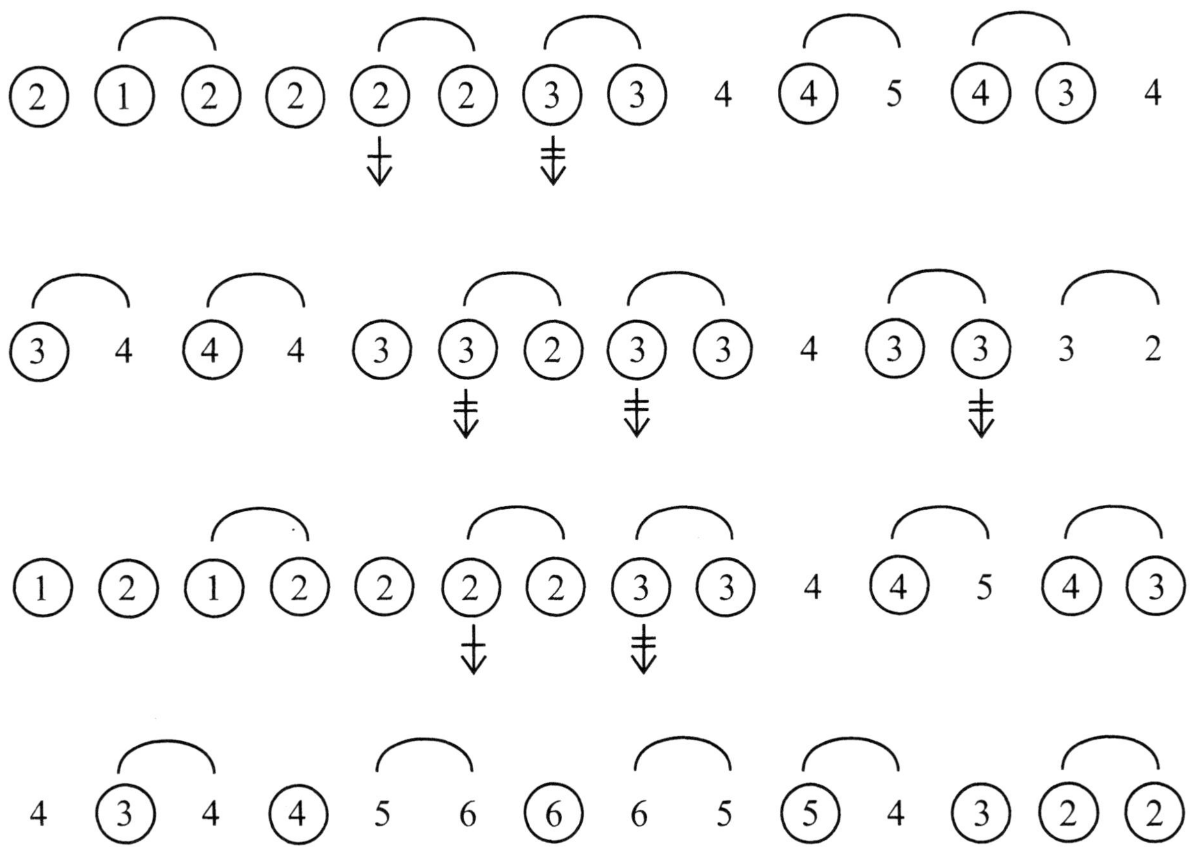

Part one repeats.
Intermediate

Part Two
D-Harp

④ 5 ⑤ 5 ⑤ 6 ⑤ 5 ④ 5 ⑤ 5 ④ ④

4 ③ 4 ④ 4 ③ ③ 3 ③ ③ 4 ③ ③

3 2 ① ② ① ② ② ② ② ③ ③ 4

④ 5 ④ ③ 4 ③ 4 ④ 5 6 ⑥ 6 5

④ 4 ③ ② ②

Part two repeats.

Performance at the Geo Theater in Opryland, Nashville, Tennessee.

Casey Jones

I'm using a C harp in the key of G on this tune. I learned this one at Jim McReynolds' suggestion, and then Jesse and I picked it until we came up with an arrangement. It's really a pretty strong melody on the harp.

Arrangement by Mike Stevens

C-Harp
Part One

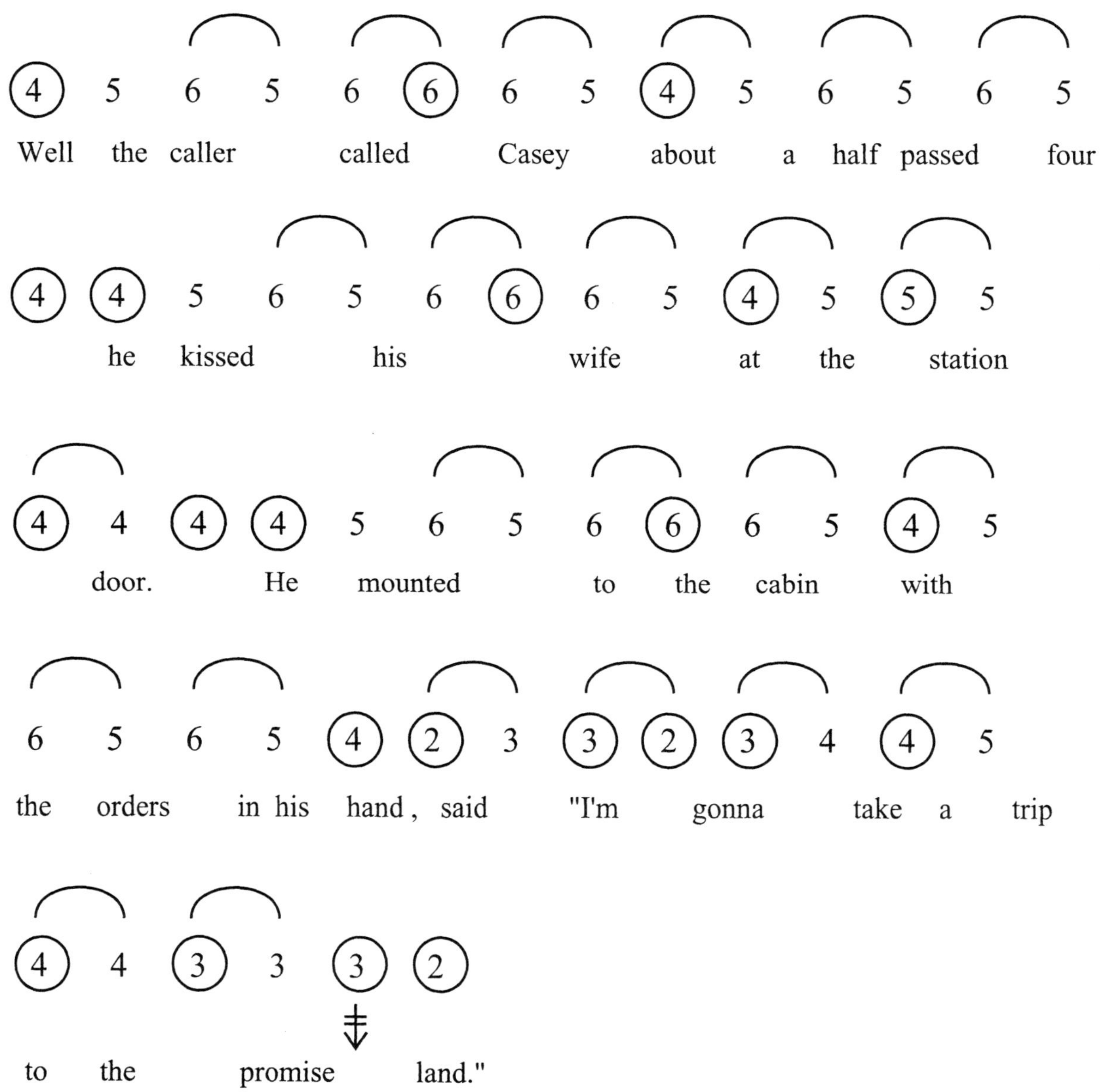

Part one repeats.

C-Harp
Part Two

(3) (2) 6 (6) (7) (6) 6 5 (4) 4

Casey Jones mounted in the cabin.

(3) (3) (2) 6 (6) (7) 6 (6)

Casey Jones orders in his hand.

(3) (2) 6 (6) (7) (6) 6 5 (4) 4

Casey Jones mounted in the cabin.

(3) (2) (3) 4 (4) 5 (4) 4 (3) 3 (3) (2)

Said, "I'm gonna take a trip to the promise land."

Part two repeats.

DeFord Bailey, the first black musician to play the harmonica at the Grand Olde Opry.

Salt Creek

Now here's a tune from my old days of playing. This solo was really developed from endless all night jam sessions at bluegrass festivals. I'm using a D harp in the key of A for this. This solo came to be because it always seemed to work and it could be played at pretty loud volume.

Arrangement by Mike Stevens

Part One
D-Harp

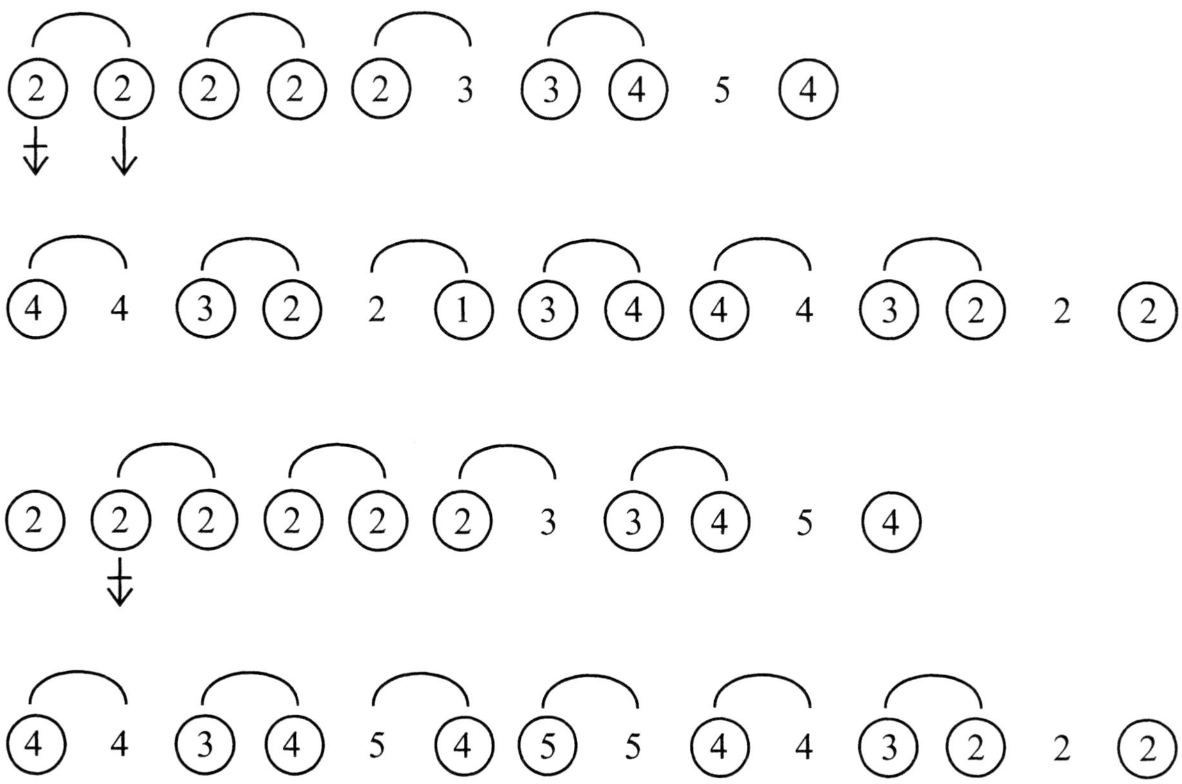

Clownin' around with Little Roy Lewis.

Part Two
D-Harp

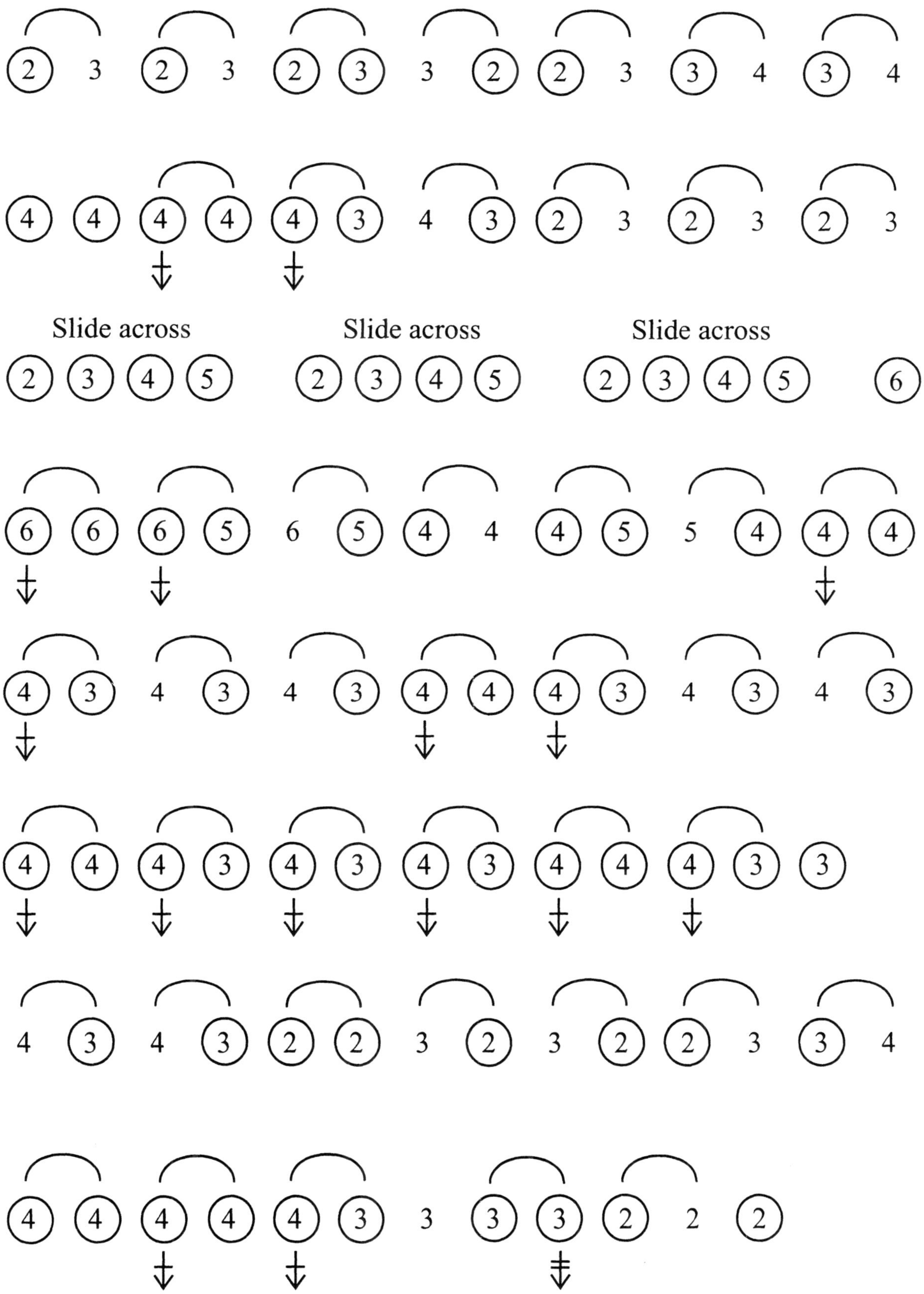

Bill Cheatum

You're gonna need some lungs for this one. This is pneumatic fiddle at its finest. It's in the key of A and I'm using a D harp.

I remember learning this tune playing with a bluegrass band called White Water Bluegrass from St. Thomas, Ontario, Canada. We ended up winning most promising new bluegrass band at the Central Canadian Bluegrass Awards, pneumatic fiddle and all.

Arrangement by Mike Stevens

D-Harp
Part One

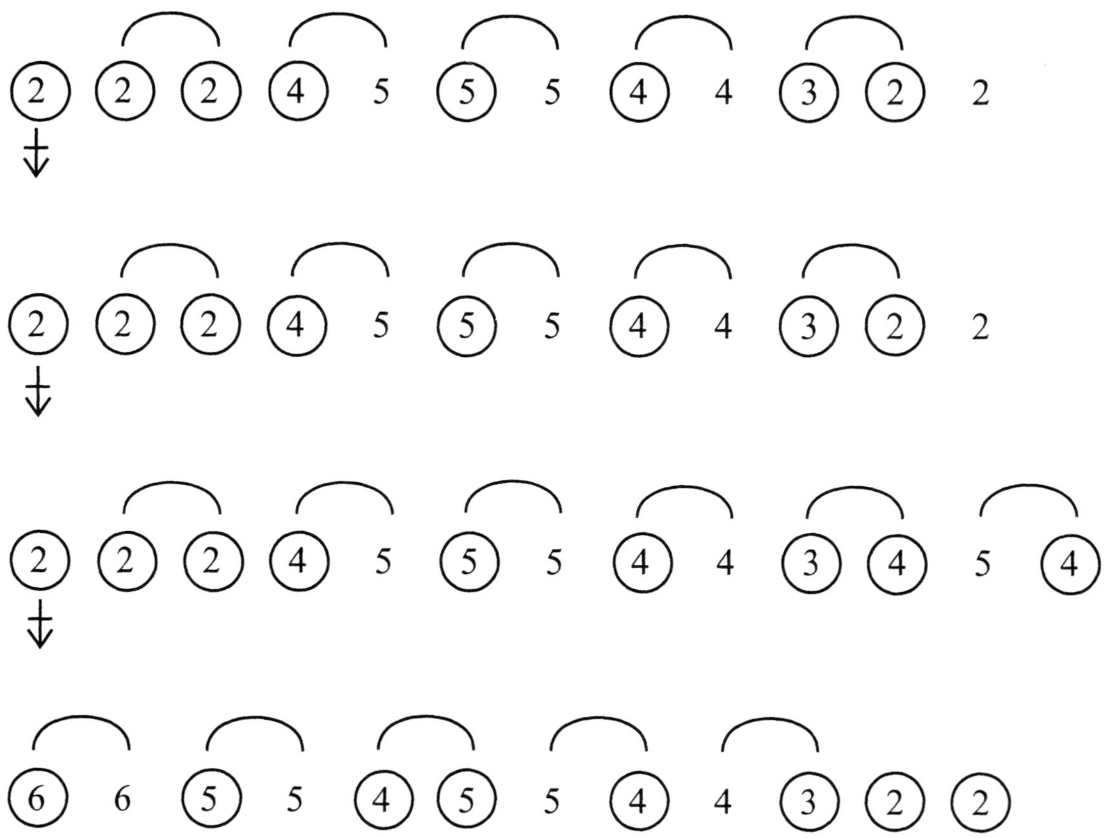

Part one repeats.

D-Harp
Part Two

(4) 5 (5) 5 (4) (5) 5 (4) (5) 5 (4) (5) 5 (4)

(4) 5 (6) 6 (5) 5 (4) (5) 5 (4) 4 (3) (2) (2)

(2) 3 (3) (4) 5 (4) (5) 5 (4) (5) 5 (4) (5) 5 (4)

(4) 4 (4)↓ (4) 4 (4)↓ (4) 4 (3) 3 (3)↓↓ (2) 2 (2)

Part two repeats.

Jesse McReynolds, Myself and Little Roy Lewis playing in Mexico.

The Big Pig Jig

This is an original tune with a major story behind it. One time while playing in Mexico with Jim & Jesse; Blaine Sprouse, Warren Blair and myself had a day off, so we ended up sampling the local activities. It turns out we had so much fun I decided to climb up on the roof of an open air restaurant and get my picture taken with this big old cement pig. Turns out the cement pig was clay and when I put my arms around it, it exploded sending me down the roof, and the rest of us almost to a Mexican jail. Many chiropractor visits later, this tune fell out.

Have fun!

Author: Mike Stevens

C harp - Think pork rinds

Part One

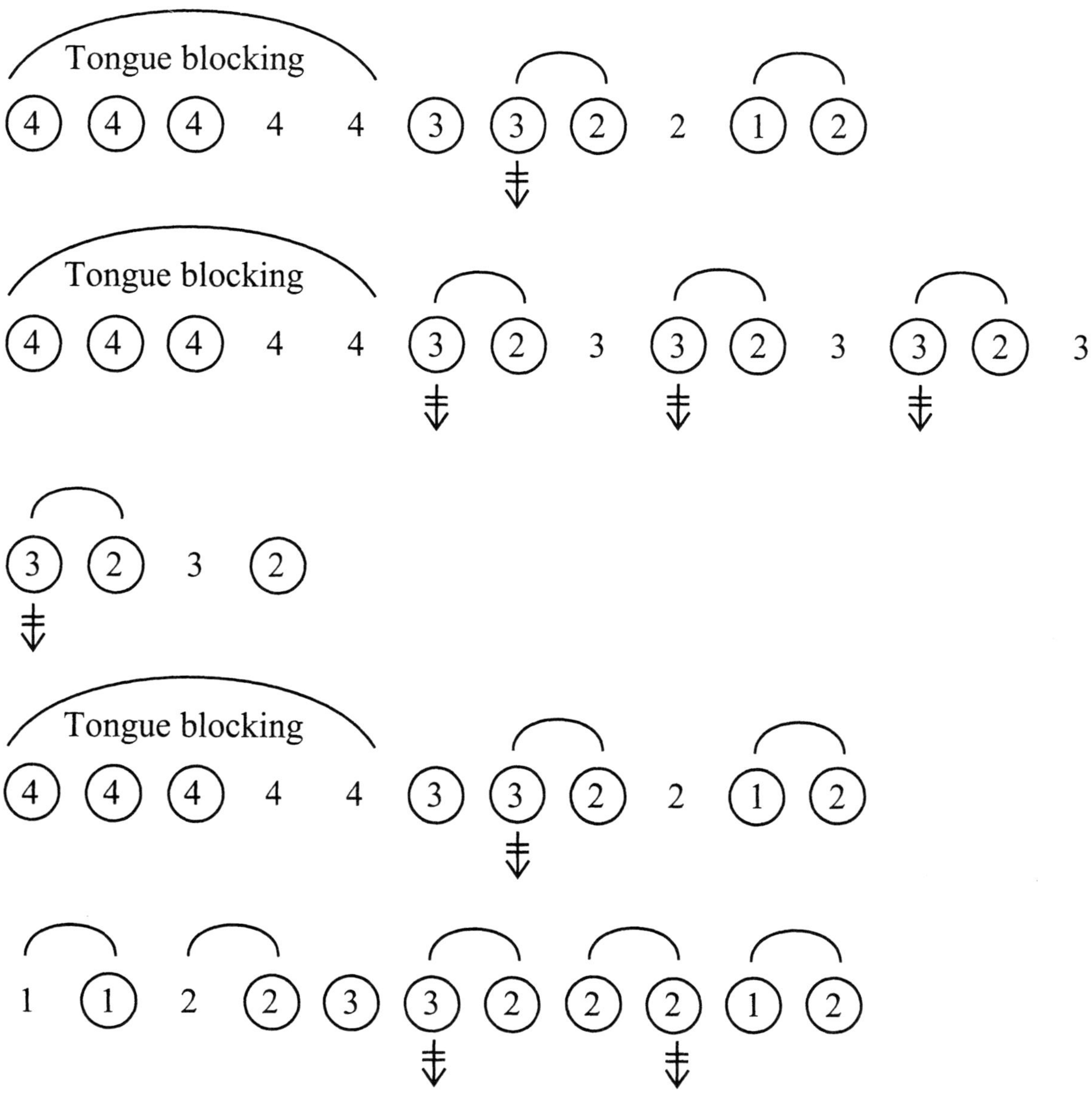

Part one repeats.

C-Harp
Part Two

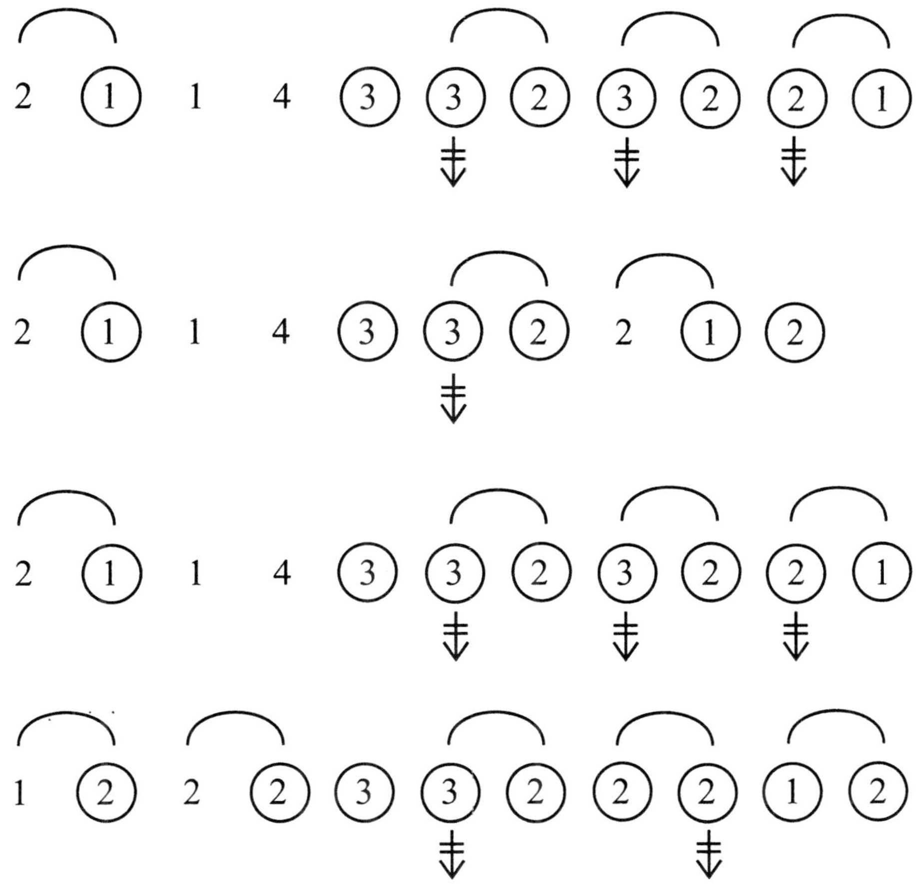

Blain Sprouse, Mike Stevens, Porter Wagoner, Jim and Jesse, and Raymond McLain.

Buggy Full Of Gnomes

I'm using a D harp on this tune. It's another original. It will help your playing because of the jumps you need to play it.

My good friend Doug Hutchens inspired this tune. It seems he was playing in a bluegrass band and had a gig in California, where the huge sequoia trees are. He had just flown there from Virginia and arrived in the early morning hours at the festival site. He found a picking session still going beside one of the huge trees. Out of the corner of his eye he spotted some people in a golf cart darting amongst the huge trees. Thus the title.

Author: Mike Stevens

D-Harp
Part One

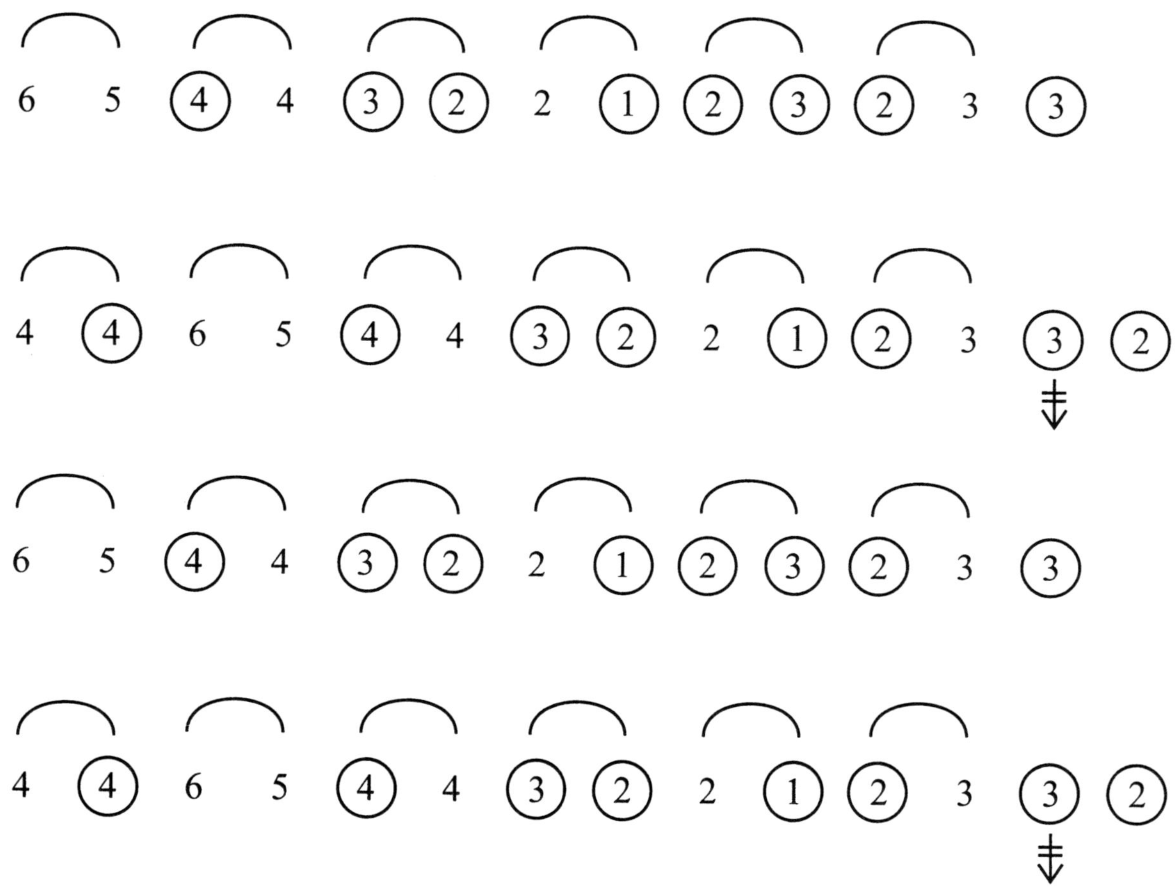

D-Harp
Part Two

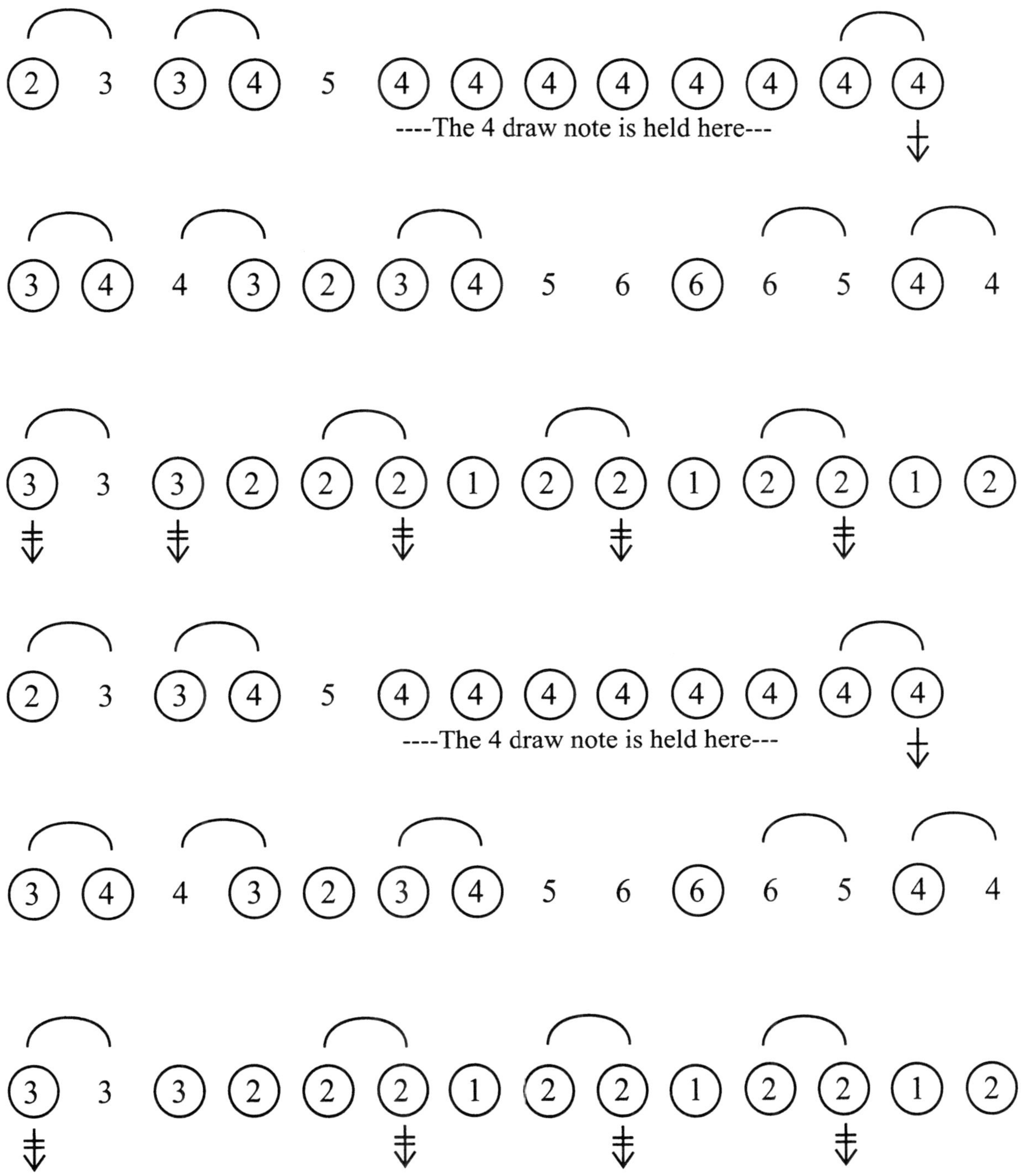

Part one repeats.

D-Harp
Part Three

④ ④ ⑤ ③ ③ ③ 4 ④ 4 ③ ②
↓ ⇊

④ ④ ⑤ ③ ③ ③ 4 ③ ② ②
↓ ⇊

④ ④ ⑤ ③ ③ ③ 4 ④ 4 ③ ②
↓ ⇊

① 2 3 ③ ③ 4 ③ 3 ③ 3 ③ ②
⇊ ⇊ ⇊ ⇊

Part three repeats.

The first time the Lewis Family called me out on stage. Carlisle, Ontario, Canada.

GRAND OLE OPRY

BLUEGRASS & GOSPEL

Spectacular

featuring

Jim & Jesse and the Virginia Boys

Mac Wiseman

CELEBRATING 50 YEARS IN COUNTRY MUSIC

FRI.-MAR. 26

7:30 P. M.

Mike Stevens WORLD'S GREATEST HARMONICA PLAYER

APPOMATTOX

HIGH SCHOOL AUDITORIUM

Sponsored by Appomattox Athletic Booster Club

ADM.: $8.00 Advance - $10.00 at door - CHILDREN ½ price

Train 45

This banjo tune has all the building blocks in it you will need to play tunes like Orange Blossom Special and Foggy Mtn Breakdown.

Take some time with it and really concentrate on the patterns I'm playing. I'm using an E harp in the key of B on this tune.

When I recorded this tune on my first record, I had played so hard I actually had bruises on my face. Also, I had to tape my headphones on so they wouldn't fly off. Give her a whirl.

Arrangement by Mike Stevens

E-Harp
Part One

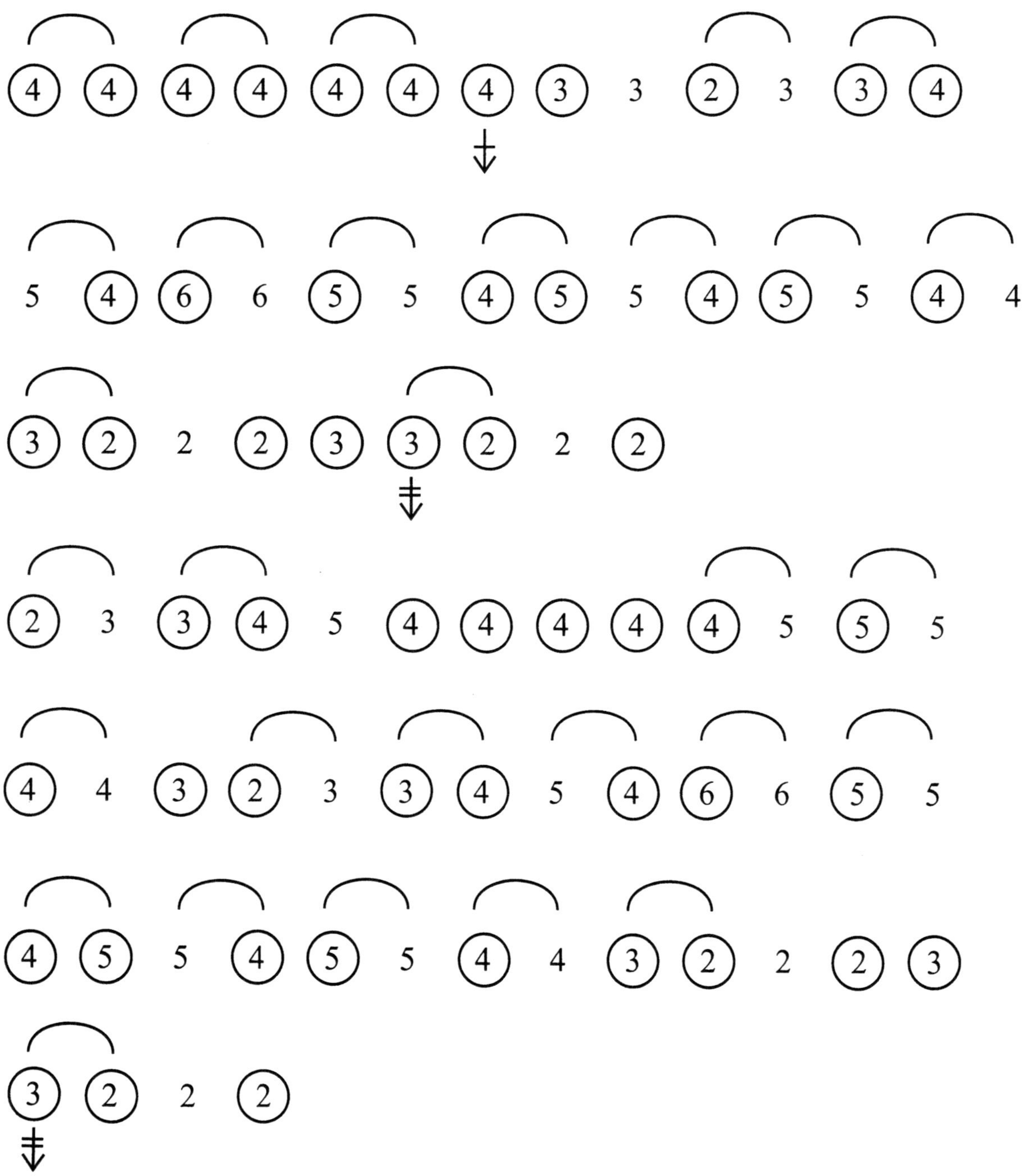

E-Harp
Part Two

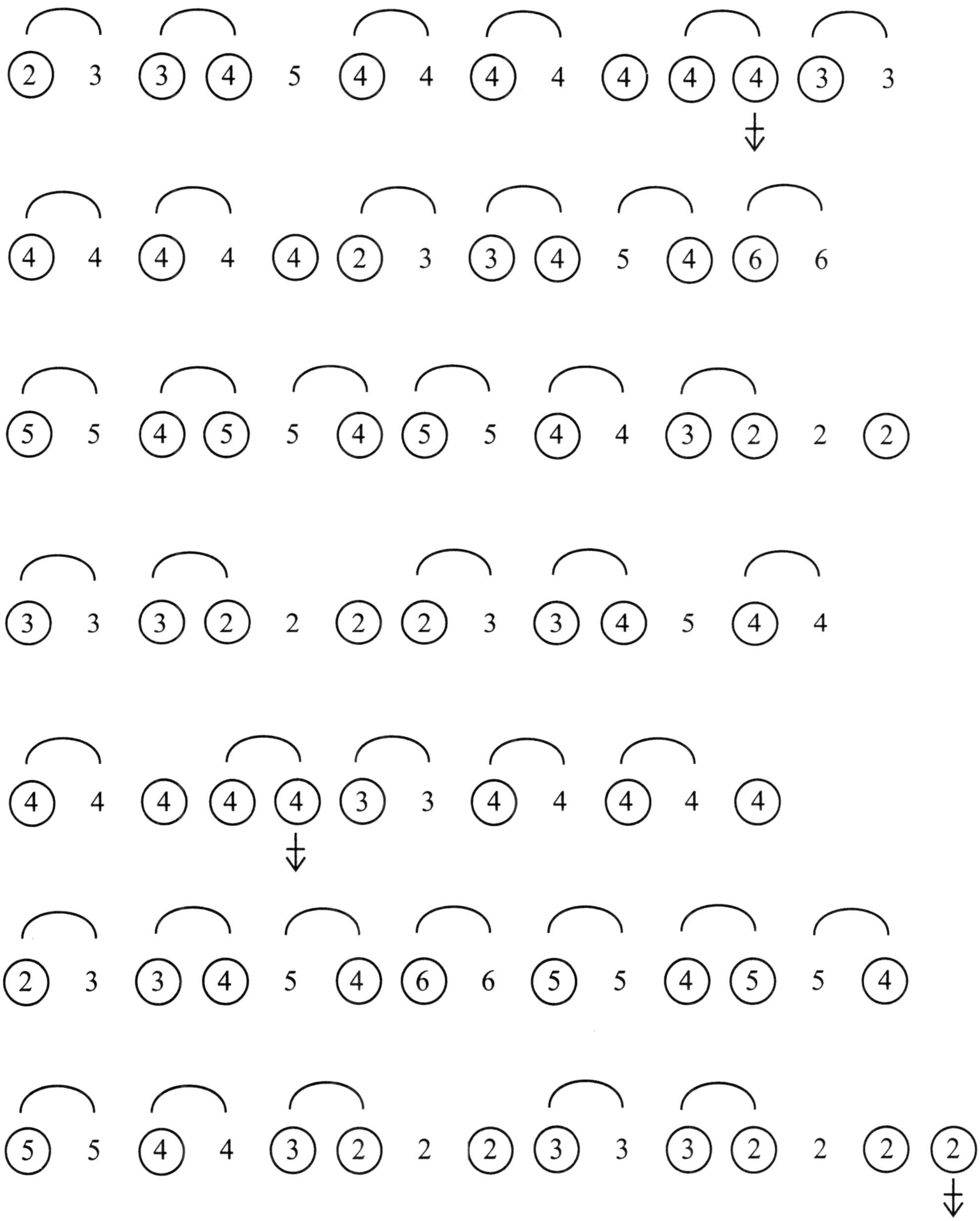

Grasshopper

This is a tune that Jesse McReynolds and I wrote a couple of years back. You will need a D harp. The single notes in the upper register will really give you a workout. On the actual recording it gets sped up about twice this speed and then played in unison. Hope you like it.

Authors: Jesse McReynolds
Mike Stevens

D-Harp
Part One

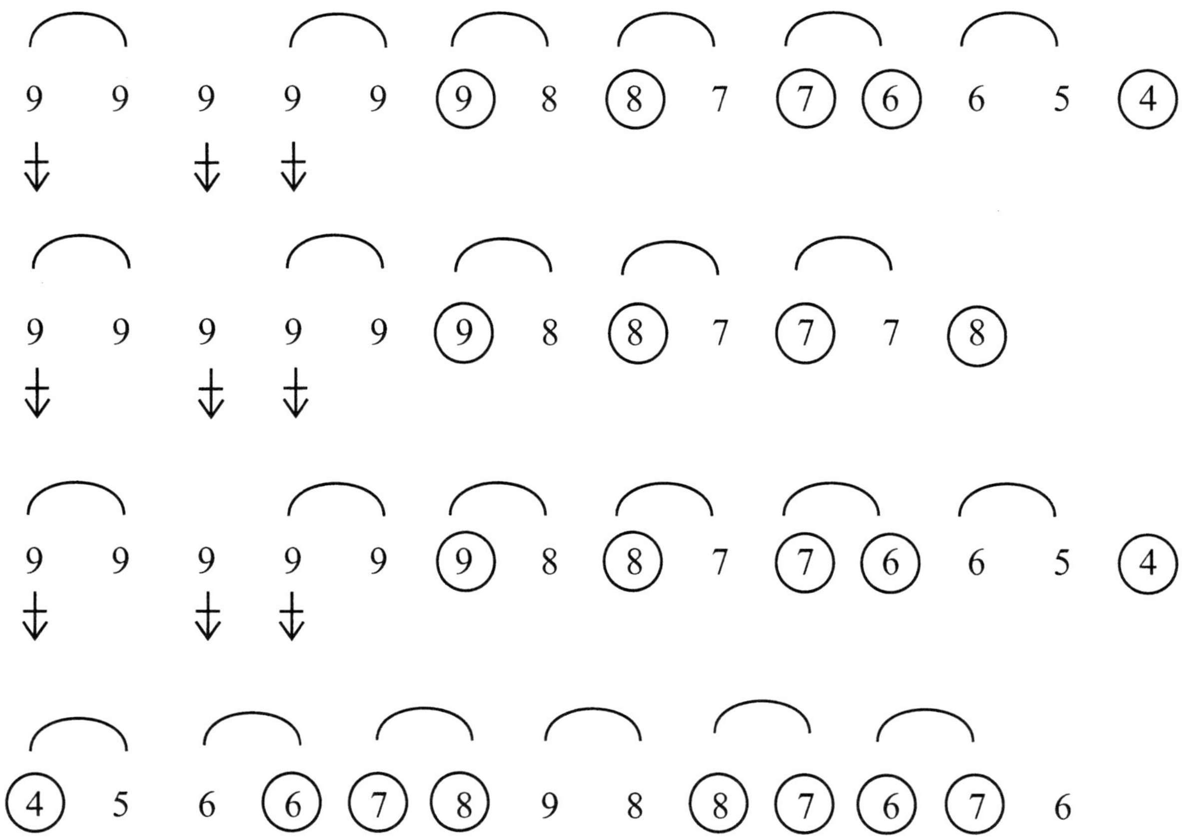

Part one repeats.

D-Harp
Part Two

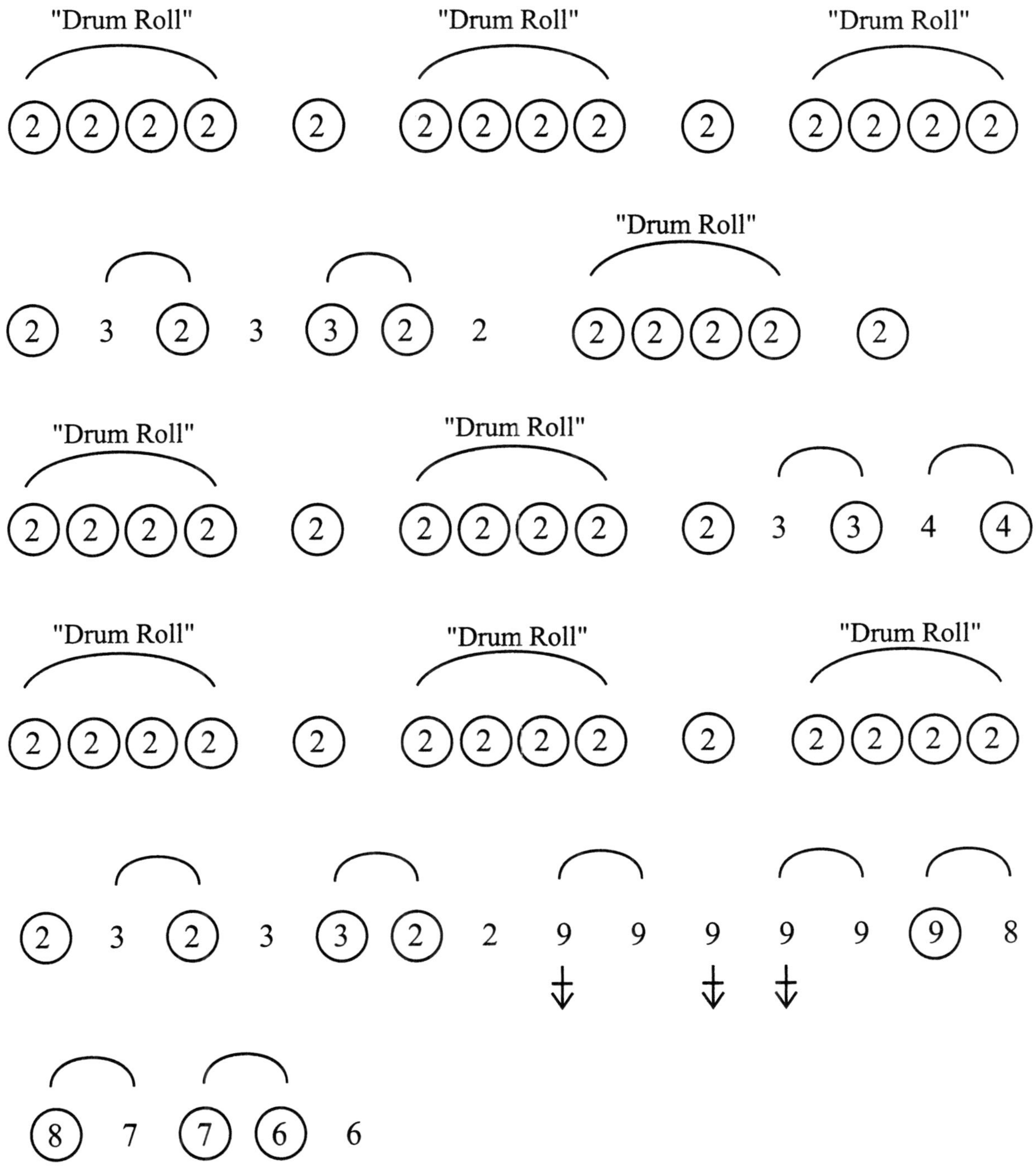

Part two repeats.
Advanced

Watermelon Pie

I'm using a D harp tuned to Am for this tune. It is one that I have written. You can also play this with a C harp in 4th position if you like.

I wrote the melody on New Year's Day, very early in the morning. I think my wife thought the rest of the year was going to be like this. It was!

P.S. If you are going to make watermelon pie, leave the seeds in.

Am-Harp
Intro.

Author: Mike Stevens

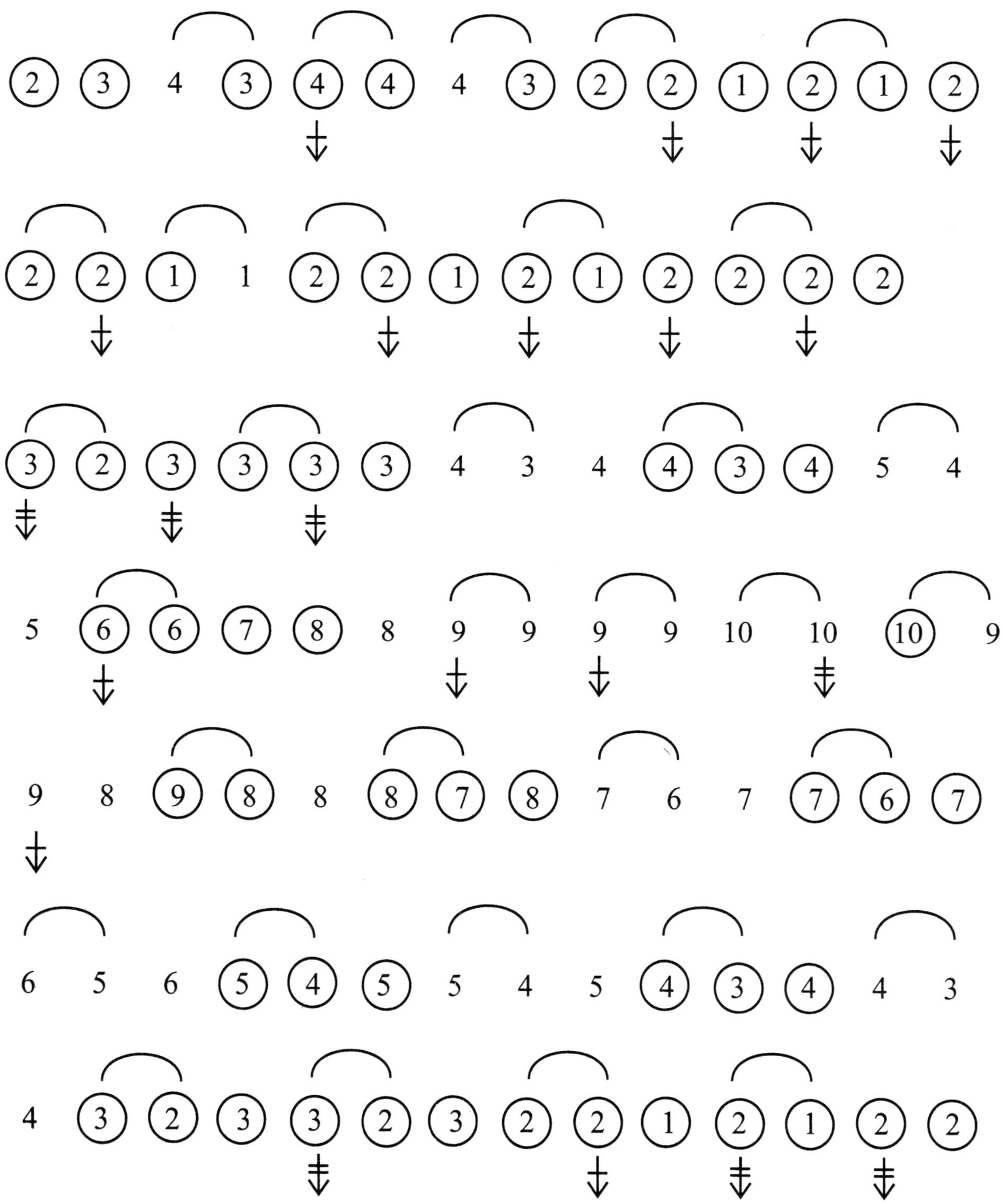

Am-Harp

Part One

② ② ③ 4 ④ 5 ⑤ 5 ④ 4 ⑤ 5 ④ 4

④ ③ ③ 4 ③ ② ① ② ② ③ 4 ④ 5

⑤ 5 ④ 4 ⑤ 5 ④ 4 ④ ③ ③ 4 3 2

Part Two

⑤ ⑤ 5 4 ④ 5 ④ 5 5 5 4 ④ 4

⑤ ⑤ 5 4 ④ 5 ④ ③ ④ 4 ④ 4 ③ ②

⑤ ⑤ 5 4 ④ 5 ④ ⑤ ⑤ 5 4 ④ 4

⑤ ⑤ 5 4 ④ 5 ④ ③ ④ 4 ④ 4 ③ ②

Copperhead Stomp

This tune I have written on a C harp. It has some simple overblows in the melody. To me it's like Ralph Stanley meets Son House.

It really shows the connection for me between delta blues and bluegrass. Incidentally, I am forever grateful that the Copperhead we are talking about here was a music lover.

Author: Mike Stevens

C-Harp
Intro.

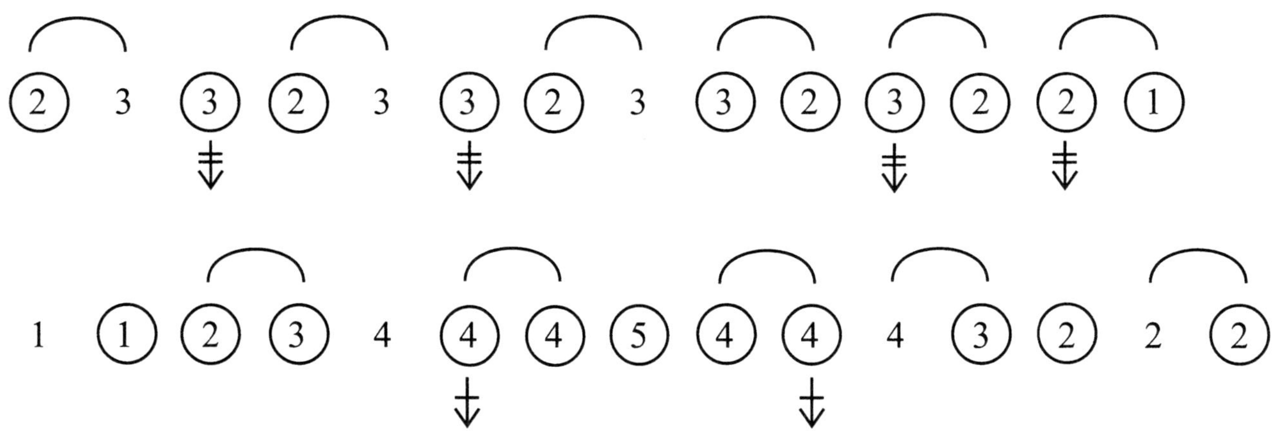

Part One

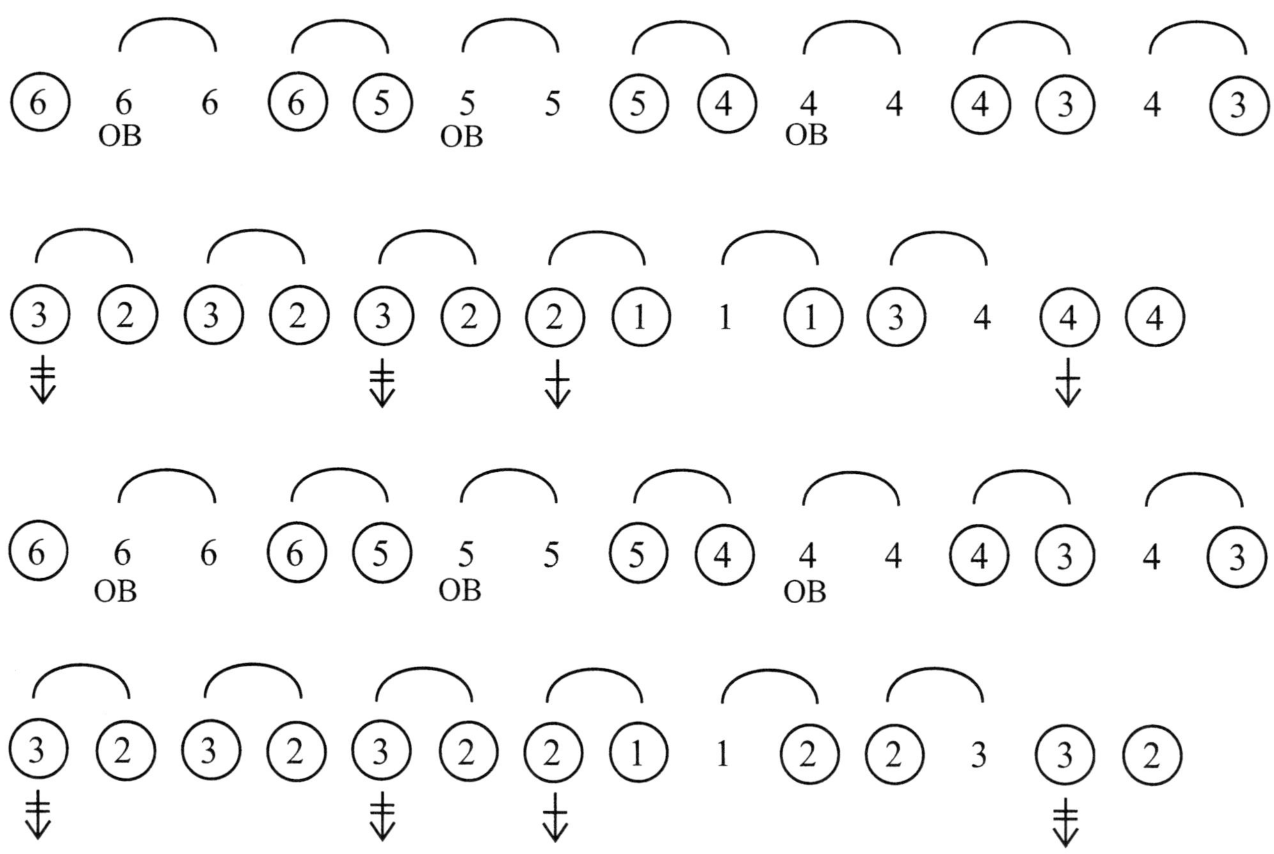

Part one repeats.

Part Two
C-Harp

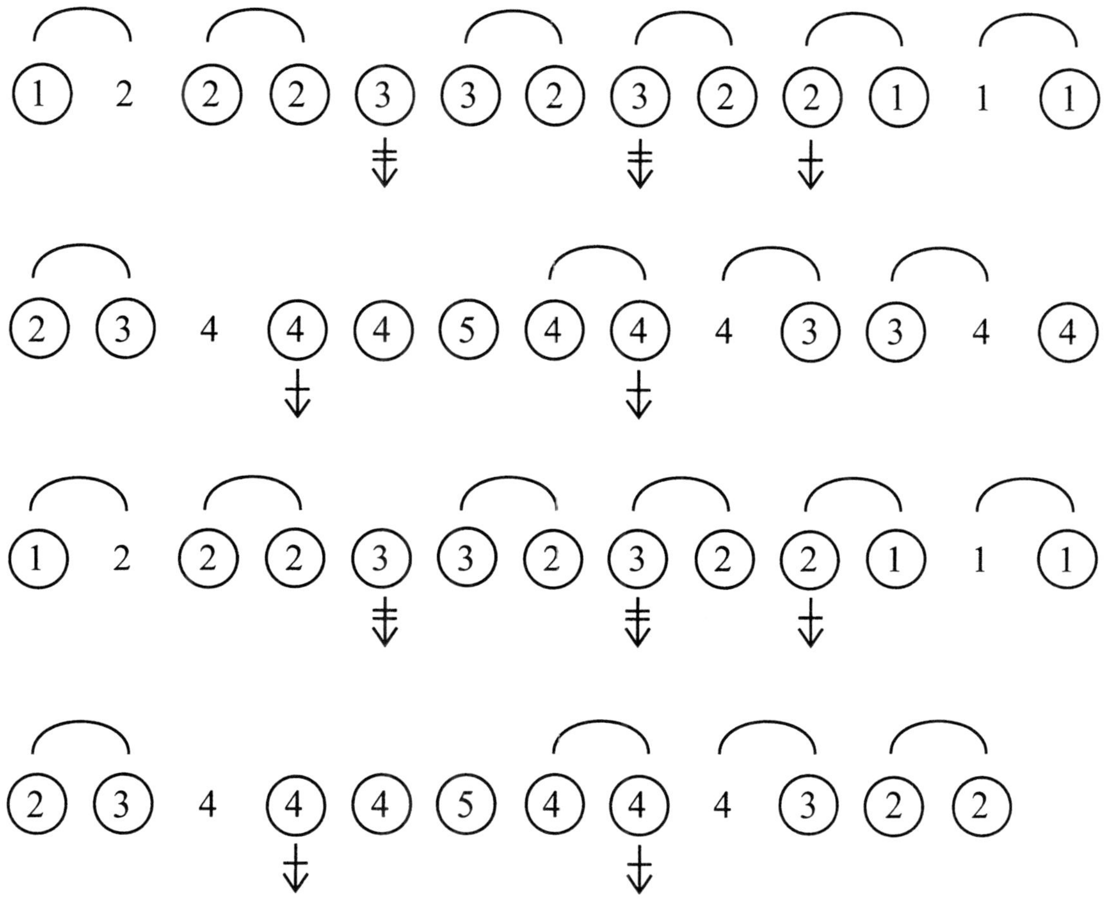

Part two repeats.

Backstage at the Opry. When Bill Monroe says, "get your harp out and try this", you get your harp out.

Colin's Cross

For a couple of weeks I went through a period of practicing only to Dizzy Gillespie records and trying to play everything on a C harp. During a break in the practicing, I was looking out the window and this whole melody came to me.

It turned out to be a sort of Celtic tune. I have no idea why, but Dizzy was definitely the inspiration for the tune.

I named it after my son Colin. When he was baptized they put a cross on his forehead and it stuck with me, thus Colin's Cross.

P.S. This one shows that there are no boundaries with the diatonic harp. The only thing stopping you is yourself.

C-Harp

Author: Mike Stevens

Part One

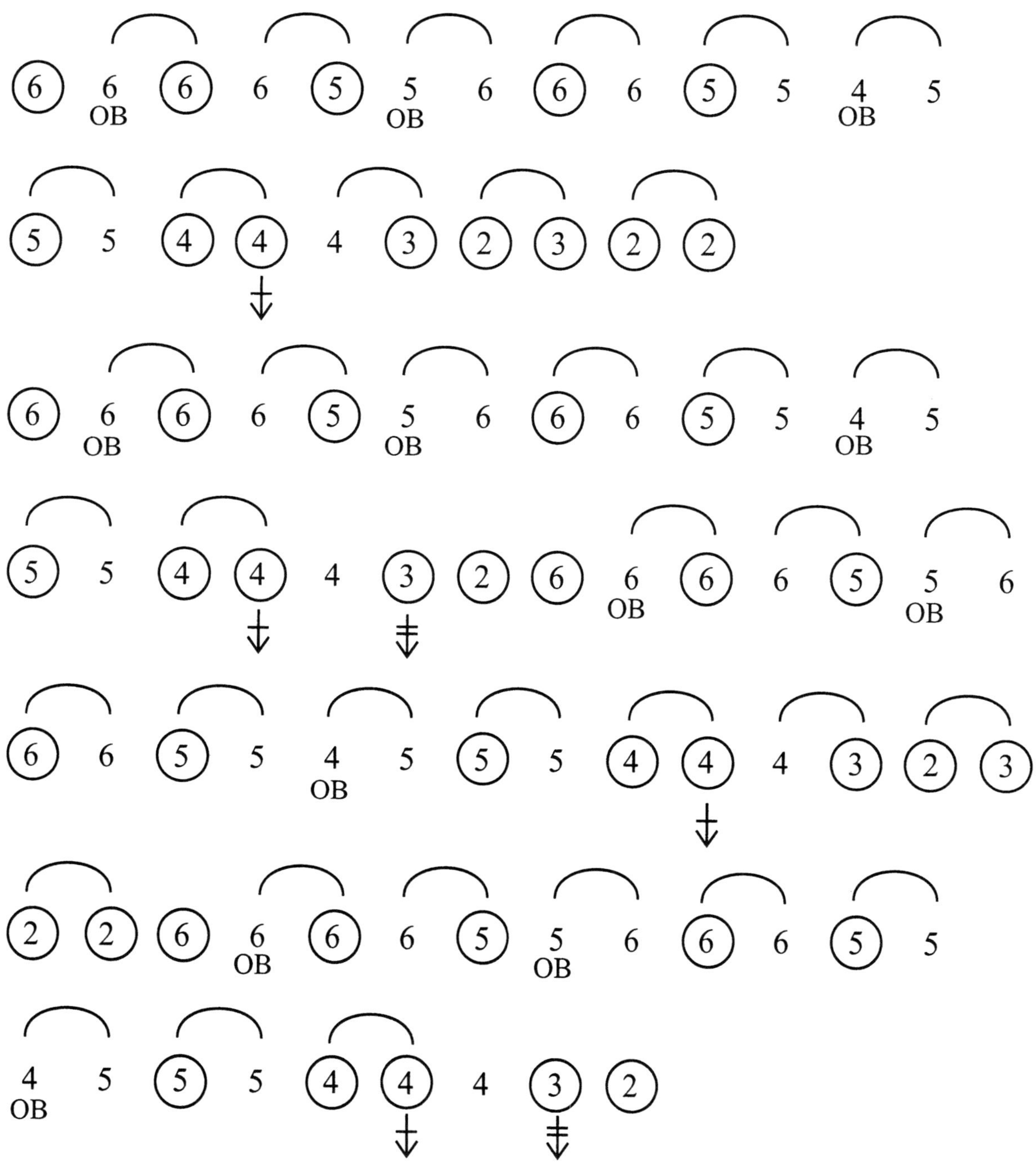

C-Harp
Part Two

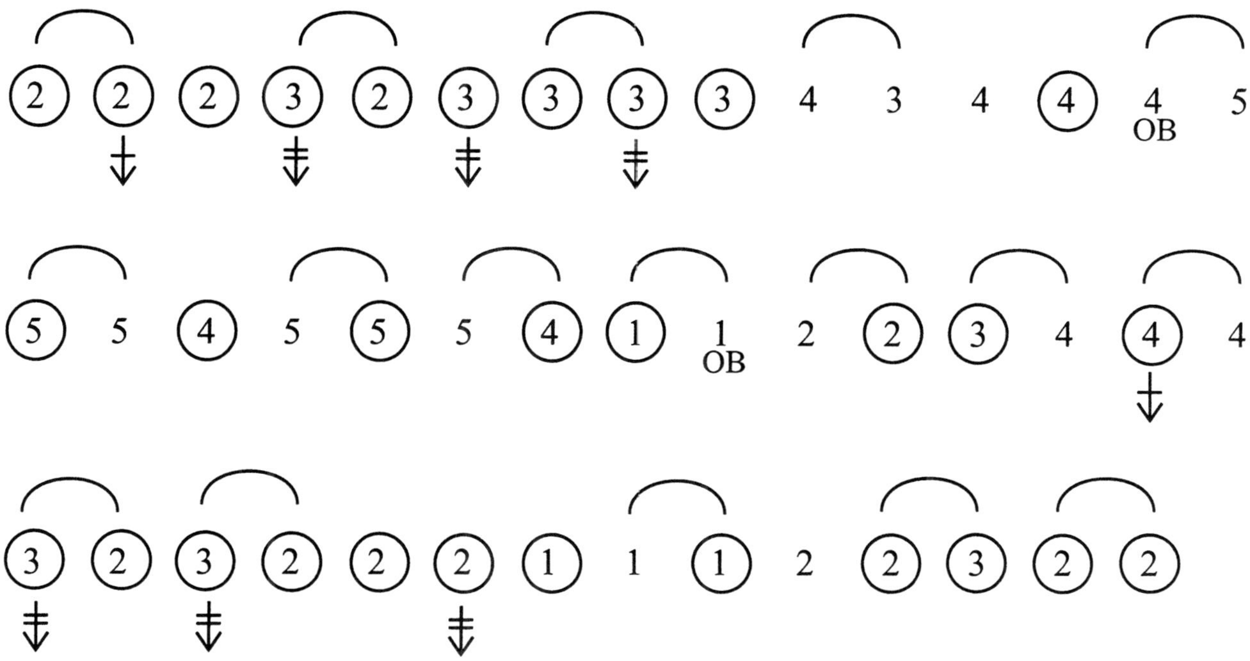

Part Three.

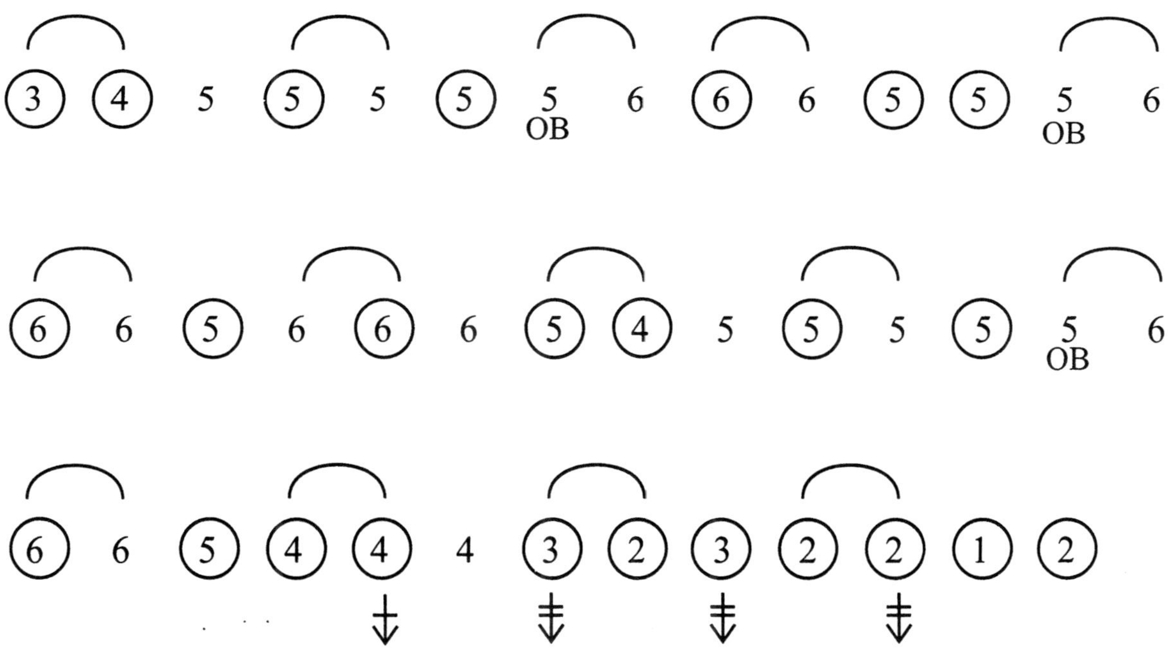

Part two repeated here.

Jesse's Request

I'm playing this melody on a C harp that I have tuned to Gm. It is a tune I've written that has a haunting melody and it sounds really good on solo harp.

Like the title says, it's dedicated to Jesse McReynolds.

Author: Mike Stevens

Gm-Harp
Part One

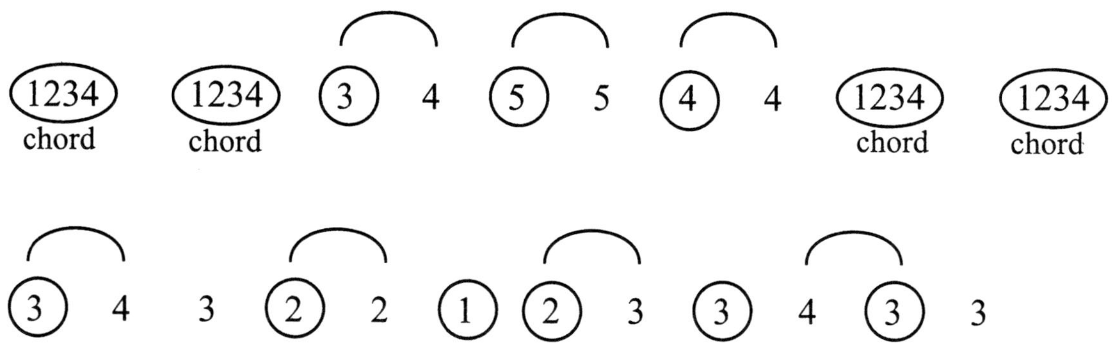

Part one repeats.

Part Two

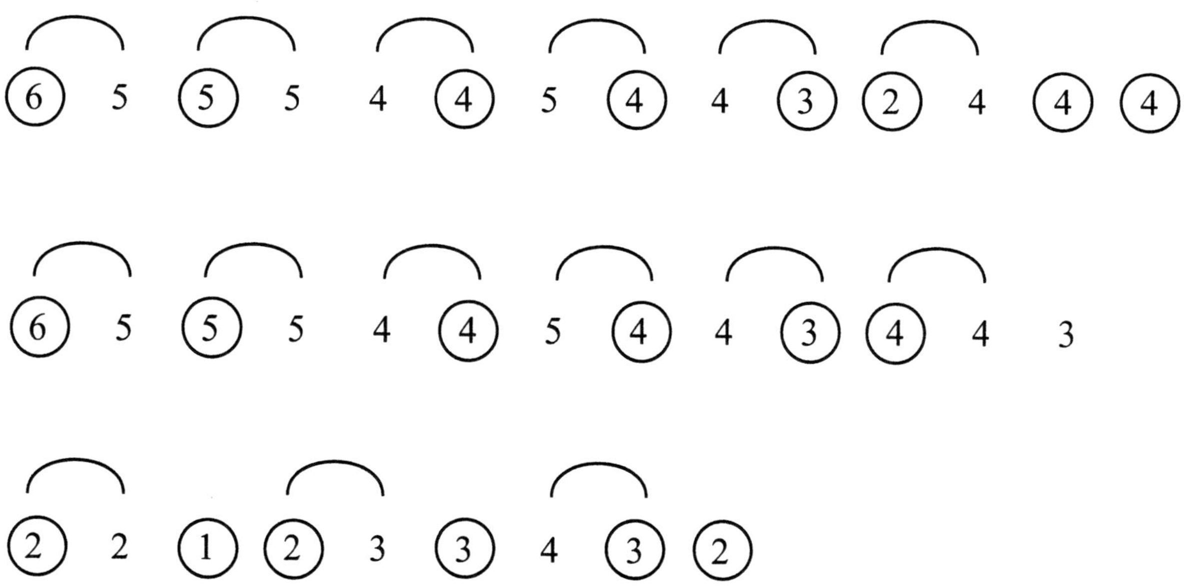

Jim and Jesse, Raymond McLain and me outside the Grand Ole Opry House.

The last of my 4th record. Michael McLain, Jesse McReynolds, Jimmy C. Newman, me and Colin, Glen Duncan, Missy Raines, Bil Vorndick and Raymond McLain.

Back stage at the Opry with Roy Acuff.

Some Things That Have Helped Me

My real influences early on were all blues players. I always could feel what they played. Some of my early influences were:

Bluegrass

Sonny Boy Williamson #2 (Harp)
James Cotton (Harp)
Paul Butterfield (Harp)
Flatt & Scruggs
Bill Monroe
Jim & Jesse
The Lewis Family
The New Grass Revival
David Grisman
The Dixie Flyers (early on this Canadian bluegrass band had a great harp player named Willie P. Bennett who played on a couple of their records).
Dave Evans
The Lost and Found

Blues

Son House
Mississippi Sheiks
Bukka White
Sonny Terry and Brownie McGee (Harp)

The harmonicas that I am playing as of this writing are in my opinion the best I've ever played. They are Marinebands that have been rebuilt and adjusted by someone who is a real genius. His name is Joe Filisko. He builds many varieties of custom harmonicas and I believe his work is a very important part of my current sound. You definitely need to contact him for any repairs, adjustments or harmonicas you might need, as I think he is the best. His current address is:

Filisko Harmonicas
1313 Cororado Ave.
Joliet, IL
60435-3704
PH 815 725-9095 FX 815 725-9097

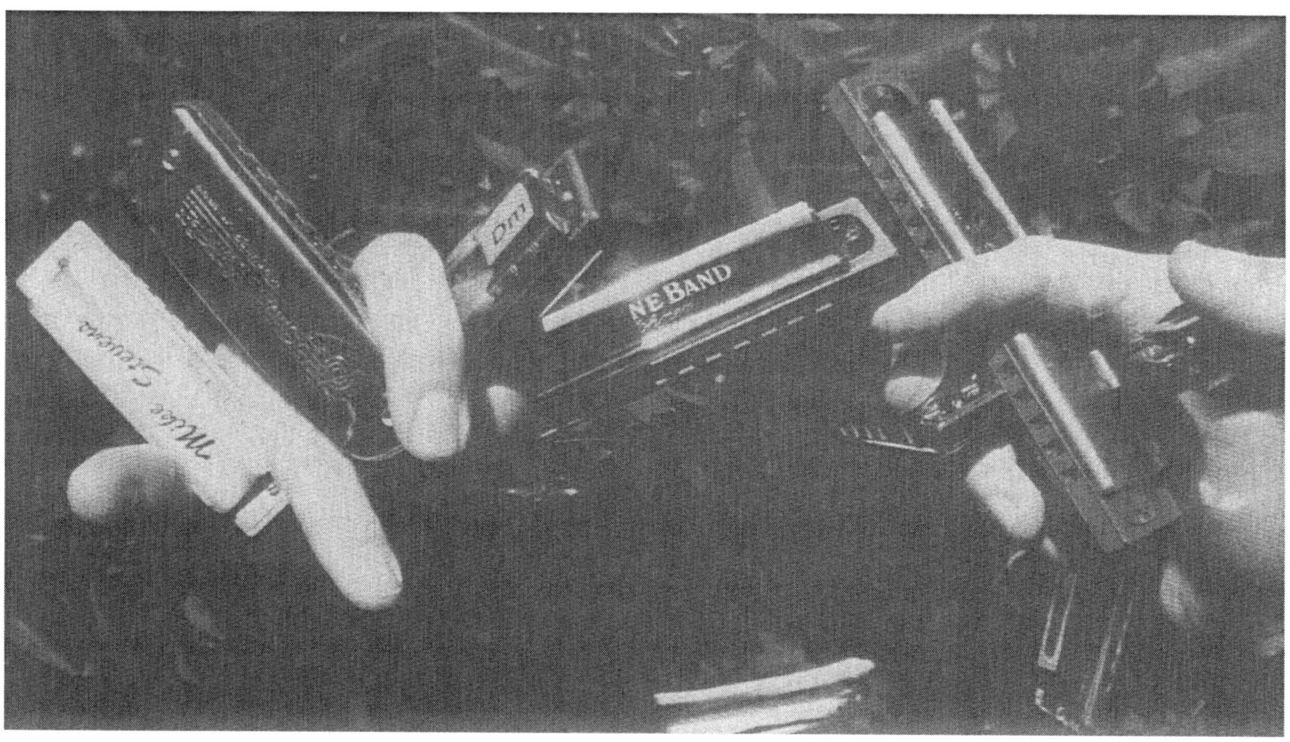

Also, I am very fortunate to get to play with a bluesman named Robert Jones from Detroit. He is the real thing. I have learned a lot from him. He is as traditional as Bill Monroe or Son House and has the same honesty in his music.

I could write a whole book on how Jim & Jesse have helped me. They are truly legends and I am honored to call them my friends. They really have a particular sound that they have developed over the years and it was a very progressive thing to bring the harp into that sound. I think it is the ultimate compliment to them that they can be considered traditional and yet continue to be innovators. I owe them everything.

Also, Little Roy Lewis and The Lewis Family, who made it their goal to get me in front of the bluegrass world. Thanks.

The Lost and Found - once at a time when I was going to give up on bluegrass and just play blues, they gave me that push to keep going. Thanks.

Finally, all the bluegrass fans who have supported me by attending the festivals and buying my recordings. Thank you.

Mike Stevens with Jim and Jesse.

Great Harmonica Music from Mike Stevens

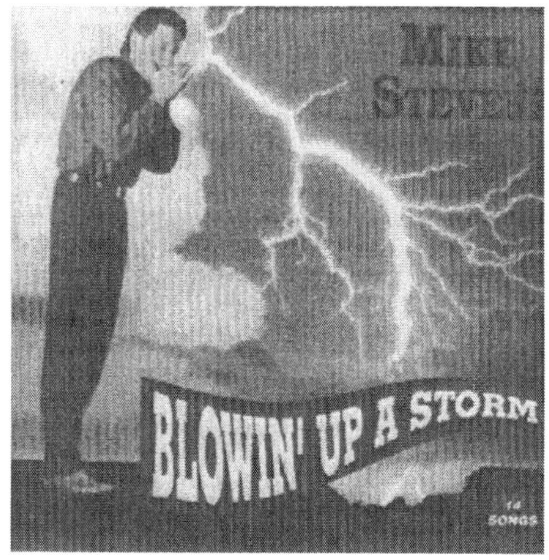

"Life's Railway To Heaven"
Down By The Riverside
This Train
Sweet Hour Of Prayer
Swing Low Sweet Chariot
When They Ring Those Golden Bells
I Saw The Light
When the Saints Go Marching
How Great Thou Art
Life's Railway To Heaven
He's Got the Whole World In His Hands
Why Me Lord
I'll Fly Away

"Normally Anomaly"
Decaf
Purple Di Di
Electric Pig Jig
Taxman Boogie
Strange Birds
Tiltin' Your Kilt
Chemical Valley Sounds
A Walk In My Dream
Canada Day
Left Lone People
Gila Babi
Rust Belt Nocturne
Critical Speed
Two Rainbows

"Blowin Up A Storm"
Pan American
Lee Highway Blues
Ghost Riders in the Sky
Whammer Jammer
Fox Chase
Ida Red
Shenandoah
Cajun Fiddle
Blowin Up a Storm
Milk Cow Blues
Black Cat
Buggy Full of Gnomes
Big Leg Women
Summertime

"Colins Cross"
Shenandoah Valley Breakdown
Listen To The Mockingbird
I'm Walking
The Chicken Reel
Casey Jones
Copperhead Stomp
Diggy Liggy Low
Grasshopper
Blues Stay Away From Me
Colins Cross
The Wreck Of The Edmund Fitzgerald
Big Pig Jig

"Harmonica"
Watermelon Pie
Foreign Accent
Salt Creek
Train 45
Amazing Grace
Red Haired Boy
Orange Blossom Special
Sentimental Journey
Bill Cheathum
Fat Lips
Foggy Mtn Breakdown
Jesse's Request

All inquiries or orders can be made to:

Mike Stevens Music
1595 Blackwell Rd Sarnia
Ontario Canada
N7X 1A4

DeFord Bailey holding a photo of Mike Stevens

From a very early Harmonica ad, circa 1930's